FROM THE

Soldiers' letters to the North East and the Borders 1914 & 1915

©Imperial War Museums (CO 2533)

Edited by BDHH, Belford

CONTENTS

INTRODUCTION

Early in 2014, Belford and District Hidden History Museum took the decision to commemorate the First World War by mounting a rolling programme of exhibitions, looking at the impact of the war on the area and its people year by year. We were fortunate in having and being given memorabilia from the War for our collections. Events at home were recorded in such things as surviving posters, certificates, newspaper cuttings and school log books. The formal record of soldiers' service could be traced through regimental diaries and histories, but these provided little detail of the day to day experiences of the Tommies. It was while looking for such stories that we discovered the rich seam of letters sent by serving soldiers to family and friends in the North East and the Borders, and published in the local press. This small book is made up of a selection of excerpts from these letters, which hopefully reflect the wide range of situations and emotions which these young men experienced.

THE WESTERN FRONT 1914 - 1915

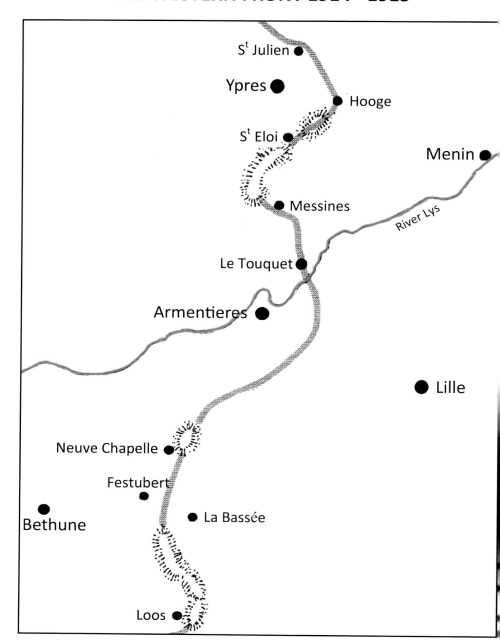

THE FIRST MONTHS OF THE WAR

Britain entered the First World War at midnight on the 4th of August 1914. Immediately the regular army, the British Expeditionary Force (B.E.F.) was mobilised and sent to France to help defend Belgium from German attack. Also called up were ex- soldiers and British soldiers serving elsewhere in the world, so that after the B.E.F. itself, some of the first soldiers to arrive in France were the British officer led Indian regiments.

The first major engagement took place at the Belgian town of Mons on 23 August 1914. Although initially a success for the B.E.F., the unexpected withdrawal of the French troops resulted in the British forces having to make a two week retreat to the outskirts of Paris, before counter-attacking on the Marne, and continuing on to the Aisne, La Bassee and Messines, as the army raced against the Germans to seize control of the Channel ports. By the end of October, both armies were digging in around the Belgian town of Ypres, which was to remain a focus of fighting for much of the war.

MONS AND THE RETREAT FROM MONS

We had a seventeen-hour sea voyage, landing at Havre. The enthusiasm in this country is extraordinary...... We remained at Havre for about two days, and then had a train journey of twenty hours to Landrecies. Thence we marched to Mons. On Sunday, the day after we arrived there, we fought our first battle, the odds in numbers being at least five to one against us. They came on in solid masses, and we mowed them down like corn. We fought again next day, and again the battle of Le Cateau on the following Wednesday I think. At the end of the first fortnight after we left Landrecies we had marched over 200 miles - 100 miles and three battles in the first week - lost 13 officers and 350 men.
I am as fit as ever. When we fought at Le Cateau we did so on an empty stomach, not having had supplies for three days. It is wonderful what one can do. We have slept all night before now in trenches full of water. I could not be happier or in better health. Don't worry about me, as I am quite safe and well, and very happy.

An unnamed young officer, letter dated 19 September 1914
Newcastle Journal 1 October 1914

Our battery had fired their last round. The Germans were only 300 yards away. The order was given, "Retire. Every man for himself." It was a splendid but awful sight to see horses, men, and guns racing for life, with shells bursting among them. The Germans rushed up, and I lay helpless. A German pointed his rifle at me to surrender. I refused, and was just on the point of being put out when a German officer saved me. He said: "'English man brave fool." He then dressed my wound, and gave me brandy and wine, and left me.

Gunner B. Wiseman, Royal Field Artillery
Newcastle Journal 26 September 1914

I was at the big fight in Mons, and it was terrible. For two days it was raining like ----- all the time with shell and bullets. We walked 323 miles in eleven days, with about two hours' sleep, and that was on the roadside. It was awful to see the men with bad feet fall at the side of the road, probably done to the world. My feet were good, but when I took my boots off one day I could not get them on, and was left on the roadside by myself.

But luck was in with me, and I met our Lancers and they let me get on a spare horse, which I had for three days. Then I met my own battalion and was all right.

Williamson, 1st Battalion Coldstream Guards
Newcastle Journal 26 September 1914

Retreat from Mons
©General Photographic Agency/Moviepix/Getty Images

have been in the firing-line since the first British shell was fired. I took part in the Battle of Mons, and our division was the one that fought the rear-guard action between Mons and Le Chateau. We were only 15 kilometres from the French capital when we started to drive the German hordes back again. Our next big engagement was the battle of the Marne. The great retirement was one of the greatest pieces of military work ever accomplished by any general. We were out-numbered by ten to one. We were next engaged in the battle of the Aisne.

I have seen enough of the Germans to state that they are hordes of beasts. They are not to be termed men; they have lost all sense of manhood and Christianity, as proved by the awful outrages they committed upon the women of Belgium. However I will leave that as it stands; but I wish the young men who have not yet enlisted to think for themselves what the Germans would do to their mothers, sister, sweethearts, wives, and children if they reached England. We left the Aisne on September 30 and went to La Bassee. We had just passed through Bethune when the enemy started bombarding it with their long-range guns. We were in the action at La Bassee and were engaged in heavy fighting and suffered heavily. At the battle of St Eloi the Germans lost about 18,000 all told. We witnessed the bombardment of Messines by the Germans with their 15 inch guns, this being the first time they had used those terrible guns since the beginning of the war. The shells caused terrible havoc wherever they dropped. After the bombardment Messines was called the "City of the Dead."

Bombardier John Gittus, 1st Brigade Royal Field Artillery
Newcastle Evening Chronicle 24 July 1915

I have seen for myself women and children horribly cut up. In one place, when we were retiring from Mons, I saw a woman lying in the street with one of her breasts cut off.

In the same place I saw children who had legs and arms cut off by the Germans. I witnessed a revolting piece of cruelty while on this march. While passing a house I heard moans as of someone in distress. With others of the company I went into the house. There we found an old man lying dead across the fireplace. But this was nothing compared with the sight which met our gaze a moment later, when, following the direction of the moans, we came upon a woman nailed to the door. Her arms were outstretched, and through each wrist a nail had been driven. The woman was alive, though unconscious, but we were not able to do anything for her until the arrival of one of the surgeon officers, under whose direction she was taken down. That woman is alive to-day, and I understand she is now in Manchester. At least she went on the boat which took a number of refugees to Manchester.

Private John Yellowley, 1st Northumberland Fusiliers
Morpeth Herald 2 October 1914

Le Cateau was a desperate affair. We were so outnumbered that each of our batteries had at least two of the enemy's batteries shooting at it. Our battery was very fortunate. We were posted behind a crest, and the enemy could not locate us. We fired over 1,000 rounds of lyddite and shrapnel slap bang into them; simply mowing them down. It is safe to say that if our army lost one man, theirs lost at least six. They came on in columns of lumps, and we had just to keep on shooting as fast as ever we could, and sometimes faster than that.

We have been advancing carefully, however, chasing the Germans by way of a change, and don't they mind. Well, in the haste of their retreat they abandoned all the cumbersome kind of articles, and we picked up such things as bicycles by the score, gramophones, concertinas, accordeons, (sic) civilian clothes, provisions of all kinds, and what not.

Our column captured some guns one day. There were a lot of dead Germans behind them. One officer was sitting quite natural, with his head resting on his hands. Another chap had evidently been a bit of a carver, for he had just finished carving a doll's house, with furniture complete. He had evidently been doing it in his spare time. Rather pathetic, wasn't it.

Gunner Thomas Trobe, Royal Field Artillery
Morpeth Herald 16 October 1914

A party of eight of the Northumberlands found ourselves in a wood, along with four men of the Royal Fusiliers and two of the Royal Scots Fusiliers. We remained in this wood for a good while, when at last we found a leader - Captain Toppin, of our regiment, who has since fallen.

He was a brave man, and worthy of the V.C. He got the little party together at the side of this wood and we saw the Germans advancing on us, so our brave leader formed us up in the open ground. Then they stopped their advance, and we were knocking them over like wooden dolls on a fair ground. We were ordered to go along by the side of the wood in single file, when a shell came over and killed our leader. We went on until we came to the end of this wood, where I found my regiment entrenching themselves, about 500 yards from the enemy's trenches.

We remained in these trenches for, I think, eight days and eight nights. What a time we had with cold and rain! It rained all the time for the eight days, and we were never dry. Sleep was impossible, and, to make matters worse, we had no overcoats or waterproof sheets. About two days before we were relieved from these trenches, we got some refreshments from England. A lance-corporal came into our trench and he had an overcoat on, and two of us got under the tails of his great-coat like young birds would get under their mother's wings.

Private H. Allport, Northumberland Fusiliers
Newcastle Journal 7 December 1914

THE FIRST BATTLE OF YPRES

I am well and in good spirits. We have got to grips with the Germans, and no mistake. I am writing under difficulties in a farm shed - we are waiting in reserve and while I write the German shrapnel shells are bursting all around us. It has been like this for days now, ever since [...] a memorable day for us for we struck the main body of the Germans. We were out on patrol, and entered a cyclist corps of the enemy near to a village. To get under cover, we had to gallop into the village under a perfect hail of bullets. The Germans were firing at us from about 300 or 400 yards, and their bullets were [striking] the road and houses which we passed. Fortunately we got through safe, but we shall never forget that gallop! We had to get into action at once and hold them until the artillery and infantry came up, which we did successfully. It was the beginning of a fierce battle, which has now lasted three days. The guns on both sides have never ceased. Last night we were shelled out of our camp, and had to retreat to a safer spot to sleep if possible. This was about 11 o'clock at night.
So far our casualties have been remarkably slight. I do not think we have had any killed, which was marvellous, as we got a lot of shelling. Our main work is going out to the flanks to help the infantry.

Trooper Harry Mattinson, Northumberland Hussars on 22 October 1914
Morpeth Herald 6 November 1914

We have had snow to-day, and things are looking very wintry, which makes one think of Christmas. We are in the line of communication, and Harry Mattison and I have been guarding a pontoon bridge which had been destroyed by the Germans. We are just behind the firing line, and I expect we are being held in reserve. We have fallen in with some nice folk here, who have allowed the two of us to come in and write our letters. They seem very fond of having a chat with us in French, and as Harry Mattison has a fair knowledge of the language, we get along immensely.
The three refugee families living here all have some miserable tale to tell about the brutalities of the Germans, who three weeks were in possession of this very house and pointed revolvers at the poor woman and made her prepare food for them. They also took some civilians from here to dig trenches for them, and

after they had dug them the Germans shot them.

Some of our men have had rather an unpleasant job during the past two days. In the villages which were considered dangerous for civilians the people were told to clear out, and our men had to go to the farms round about and see that they left and went to a place of safety. To see the refugees trudging through the snow and slush, with bundles of clothes and other little things they could carry, made one thankful that our homes are so far off and not likely to be troubled by invasion.

Trooper Henry Michie, Northumberland Hussars
Morpeth Herald 4 December 1914

I am taking the opportunity afforded by a quiet spot - it is a deserted home - to write you another letter. I am still in the danger zone, but will not worry you with any more experiences, except that I am keeping two pieces of shrapnel from a shell that blew half the house away that I was operating in. I think I am lucky enough to pick the winner of every big race after this.

I will tell you of an amusing hour I had last night. My line covers a few miles, and various other stations branch off from it. One of these was a French artillery station, and a French signaller managed to put a gramophone in position near the microphone of his instrument. The line echoed to the strains of the "Marseillaise," "Double Eagle," and "Stars and Stripes," etc. At the end of each selection a buzzing of applause from the English signallers were wafted down the line, and strangely pronounced French showed the approval, like "Bon monsieur," "Merci," and "Encore."

I was as delighted as the remainder at the "turn," and determined to go one better than my comrades. So I studied a small French handbook, and laboriously picked out what I considered a suitable sentence which would put the "Kybosh" on the Tommies' French. This is what I arrived at; "Merci, monsieur, donnez moi chante, s'il vous plait," which I translate, "Thank you, monsieur, give me a song, if you please." It got home all right, and the Frenchmen sang us some stirring melodies, to which our boys were not long in replying. One classic youth rendered something from "Il Trovatore," rather nicely. An incident like this is a pleasant relaxation from constant shell "dodging."

Private Harold Booth, Northumberland Fusiliers
Newcastle Journal 11 December 1914

CELEBRATING CHRISTMAS AND NEW YEAR

The Christmas Day truce of 1914 has gone down in legend, but depending where one was on the day, Christmas was celebrated in different ways. Less well remembered was what happened at New Year or at subsequent Christmases, but for those there, these too were memorable.

I never thought we would spend Christmas the way we did. We were in the trenches on Christmas Day. On Christmas Eve the Germans in front of us started singing what appeared to be hymns. We were shouting for encores (their trenches are only about 150 yards in front of us), and they kept the singing up all night. On Christmas Day some of them started to shout across to us to come over for a drink.

It started with one or two going over half-way and meeting the Germans between the two lines of trenches, then it got that there was a big crowd of German and British all standing together shaking hands and wishing each other a Merry Christmas. They were giving us cigars and cheroots in exchange for cigarettes, and some of them had bottles of whisky. They seemed a decent crowd that was in front of us.

They were all fairly well dressed, and the majority of them could speak broken English. Some of them could speak it as well as myself. They said they were not going to fire for three days. They kept their word, too; there was no rifle fire for two days after Christmas. There were two dead Frenchmen between our lines. We could never get out to bury them till that day. The Germans helped us to dig the grave. One of their officers held a service over one of the graves. It was a sight worth seeing, and one not easily forgotten - both Germans and British paying respects to the French dead.

Corporal Robert Renton, Seaforth Highlanders
Newcastle Journal 6 January 1915

We had a rather curious Christmas. You will be surprised to hear we left our trenches, went half way, the Germans doing the same, and had a good Christmas greeting, getting cigars and cigarettes and all sorts of presents. They think the British a very brave lot, and fairly gave us a good clapping on the back. They said they were going to keep up the truce for 3 days; and they were as good as their word; there was not a single shot exchanged on either side. We could knock about just the same as if peace was declared; in fact, some of our fellows were playing football along the firing line - rather a curious affair after such revengeful attacks on each other. They sang songs and shouted at the pitch of their voices for 2 nights. There are a great many of them who have been in England and speak good English.

A soldier in the Seaforth Highlanders writing on 28 December
Berwick Journal 7 January 1915

Christmas 1914 is now a thing of the past, but I must confess that although on active service, I along with my comrades in the detachment managed to enjoy ourselves very much. I started celebrating Christmas on the 24th. On Christmas Eve we had a musical evening. No one was downhearted at all so "King Ragtime" was re-awakened with a vengeance. Ragtime, however, didn't reign too long. We had solos, some good old fashioned songs (not forgetting the Scotch ones) and last but not least – carols. It was a time of uncertainty, none of us knew how soon we might have to move, but trust the Tommy to make the best of a bad job, or at least I should say making the best use of any opportunity such as we had.

We were determined to have some kind of Christmas celebration and we had it. However, I couldn't take too much part in the sing song as I had to commence duty at 1 a.m. on Christmas Day, so I had a little sleep before commencing, knowing full well I would stand little chance of getting any when finishing about breakfast time. I started Christmas Day very well indeed, having bacon and eggs for breakfast, the bacon we got supplied, the eggs were procured – from where I cannot say.

After breakfast we all helped to make things as comfortable as possible and then our thoughts turned instinctively to dinner. We then organised what is known to the Tommy out here as a "scrounging" expedition and by the time everyone had returned we found we could manage a very good dinner. Pork chops, potatoes and plenty of vegetables were in our possession and having the means of cooking them alright I can safely say the dinner when finished wouldn't have caused a murmur from the most severe critic.

Christmas wouldn't have been complete without a pudding, so I may mention we had Christmas pudding too. We burnt it in the customary way, wished each other compliments of the season and then – exit pudding. I don't think there was one of us who didn't feel perfectly happy after dinner. Although our surroundings were none too homely, we felt thankful for being able to get our dinner in peace. Naturally our thoughts were far away at home, wondering how our old folk were faring and doubtless wishing we had been able to fill the vacant chair which could be vividly pictured by the mind's eye. "Ah well chaps we'll be home for next Christmas" was one fellow's consoling remark, to which I heartily said "Roll on".

I was on duty again after dinner, but was fortunate enough to be present at tea time. What a revelation tea time was! Most of the fellows had had parcels from friends at home, with all manner of good things suitable for tea and so by "mucking in" (another soldiers' phrase), we had a real good "bust up" sardines, cakes, scones, butter and bread and jam were all abundantly represented so it does not need an extraordinary intelligent person to understand how much we enjoyed ourselves.

At night we had another concert, which lasted till very late at night and so ended my Christmas Day on the battlefield. It would be unfair not to mention our two officers, who, I am sure, were partly instrumental in lightening our work as much as possible so as to give us a good time. They are both "two of the best" and I consider myself extremely fortunate in having such fine fellows in charge. It is now very close to the New Year, 1914 is closing down its black and war stained pages. Let us hope that 1915 will bring us victory and that very soon we will see the tone (sic) of war closed and clasped never to open again.

Sapper W. Cromarty, 2nd Division Signal Coy., Royal Engineers, dated 30 December 1914
Berwick Advertiser 8 January 1915

I suppose you will be wondering how I spent Christmas. Christmas Eve was spent in trench-digging. I managed to buy an old hen, which I handed over to Madame Rose to cook. Christmas Day broke hard and frosty - one could not have wished for a better day. My dinner was ready at one o'clock. The old hen had been ably converted into a nice young chicken by Madame Rose, who proved a grand cook. We had it to boiled potatoes and salad, followed by a nice plum pudding sent by Mrs Cookson.

My partner, Henry Michie, was, unfortunately, on guard at a bridge three miles off; but I obtained permission and rode out with his Christmas dinner. We had the remainder of the chicken on the following day. It was beautifully tender. We played football in the afternoon. At tea time I had to content myself with bread and butter, in consequence of orders to be ready to move at any moment.

In the evening we had a "smoker" in the estaminet of the village. The colonel and officers made some fine speeches - mostly very witty - and they kept up the cheerfulness. We had songs and recitations, and then dispersed to our beds. The rats seemed to have got reinforcements, and we hear them running in the straw about us during the night. But it gives us a safe feeling, for it lets us know we are not alone. We are all keeping well and cheery, so do not fret.

Trooper Harry Mattison, the Northumberland Hussars
Morpeth Herald, 15 January 1915

We were lucky enough to be out of the trenches a few days at Christmas, and instead of being in the usual barn or mill we generally get to, we were billeted in houses, four in each house, and the civilians in our house were very good to us. You ought to see the boys trying to make themselves understood to the French. I think we'll all be Frenchmen by the time we come back. It was good to get into a soft bed, and get your clothes off - the first time since leaving Newcastle on August 4th. Think of it!

The boys in the trenches had a decent day on Christmas Day as well. There was no firing that day. At parts of the line some of them were even meeting the Germans half-way, and having a crack with them. It is great to hear the tales they are taught to believe on the other side. They told our men all sorts of news, and everything was going against us, of course. We went into the trenches again on Boxing Day, and I thought we were going to speak to the Germans as on Christmas Day. Some of our lads started shouting over to them, and very soon they were doing the same. Then one or two chanced their heads up, and before very long every one was up. In some cases one or two of our fellows were on top of the trench, and we were all whistling and shouting over to each other, but that was as far as it got. We weren't quite so friendly on New Year's Day as their snipers were all out for what they could get, but we were not to be caught on the first day of the new year, so they had no luck.

Private Frank Brown, 2nd Battalion Durham Light Infantry
Newcastle Journal 15 February 1915

When we were all asleep on New Year's morning the Germans started to fire volleys over our heads, and we thought they were on top of us. We started to fire at them until we found they were only breaking the New Year in, because they commenced singing and blowing bugles. One of them nearly came up to our trenches, and called out "A happy New Year to you all," and another shouted, "I want a [pass] for England." They wanted to roll some beer over to us, but our officer stopped them. The fellows in front never fired at us all the time, but a sniper on the right of us accounted for four of our fellows. Our trenches are good ones, they were built by the Engineers - all wood and nice and warm to sleep in at nights.

Private Tunney
Newcastle Evening Chronicle 19 January 1915

Rather are we more concerned to ... give a glimpse of Tommy's adaptability in providing his Christmas dinner. This we - our section only - had in a barn near our billet. Two of our boys had been given permission to go to the nearest town, some three kilometres off, for the purpose of purchasing fodder, and, naturally, they came back laden after having been supplied with a "Kitty" from the pockets of the section wherewith to provide the necessary provender. To begin with, we had a disappointment, as we could not get a turkey for love or money, but trust a soldier not to be beaten, for as we gazed on the substitute, behold, they held a leg of pork. It cost 26 francs! Some leg! Did I hear some thirsty nature ejaculate "drink!" if so, there were two bottles of port, two of champagne, one of red wine, and one of white wine. We went off to our "estaminet" with our victuals, and our hostess, being a sport, consented to help us on our way to a good downright Christmas dinner. To be as brief as possible, the following was our menu for the evening: Soup, (vegetable); roast pork; potatoes (boiled and chipped); haricot beans; onions (boiled) and tomato sauce; Christmas pudding and milk sauce. The latter we made ourselves with flour, butter, milk, etc., as it seemed to be a mystery to our cook. It was glorious! We then adorned the table for dessert. What a spread! Fancy a real white tablecloth, and on it spread in orthodox homely fashion, three fruit loaves (one seed); three plates of biscuits; one plate of nuts, one of almonds and raisins, one plate of chocolate, a box of figs, a box of dates, a jar of lemon cheese, two glasses for each man, bottles of wine, port and champagne, and last but not least, sundry boxes of cigarettes. Amidst it all home was not forgotten. The toast "Old Folks at Home" was drunk in champagne, and with a deep concern. We never for a moment dared contemplate such a scene on the other side, yet here it was full of meaning to the sensitive mind, if at the same time somewhat productive of a sensitive moment. Who would have thought it possible in a land laid bare and desolate by the ravages of war. Of course, the greater part of our spread was from Christmas parcels received by our sections. They were all pooled; hence, a good and strong pull (sic) paved the way for a typical Christmas dinner. Can our donors rest content with this scene, provided by their goodness? This spirit of pooling is without doubt the secret of Tommy's success; for the spirit of comradeship - nay, brotherly love - is a fact to marvel at, and is a virtue being slowly but surely developed among men who until some time ago were utter stranger to each other. War has its drastic side, but this little picture will, we hope, allay to some extent the all-too zealous and harmful anxiety as to the welfare of soldier sons abroad.

Privates J. T. Reed and Lionel Bell, Royal Fusiliers
Newcastle Evening Chronicle 29 December 1915

WAR HORSES

The popularity of Michael Morpurgo's 'War Horse' in all its various forms – book, play and film, has done much to highlight the vital part played by horses throughout World War 1. It is easy to forget, even so, that at a time when mechanised transport was still in its infancy, horses were essential not only for the cavalry, but also as transport for food munitions and the wounded across the shattered land.

Since coming out from England we have covered a tremendous amount of country, and have seen quite a lot of actual work. In fact, this division has had its work set all along. Warfare under favourable circumstances is bad enough in all conscience, but under wet, snowy, or frosty conditions it is very bad to stick. Now horses are practically no good. The land is covered with a white mantle of snow, whilst the roads are frost-bound. The horse I am riding is a beggar. It can't jump higher than a straw, and insists on standing on its hind legs or galloping with its head between its legs. However, it is only for a while, and I shall have my own back again, and he can jump absolutely anything.

Trooper James Wilson, Northumberland Hussars
Newcastle Journal 2 December 1914

I do not know if I mentioned in my last letter that my pony had been killed by a piece of shell hitting him just behind the saddle. Well, he is gone, poor beggar - the same way as many a score more. I've got a good mare now - not much of a jumper, but very fast at the gallop, which may mean much, if I have to run for it any time. I was complimented on the way I gave information respecting the locality of a battery of German guns. (Some time ago now, so I can speak of it.) The colonel wanted information from a certain sergeant and other three men who were out on patrol, but they never drew rein.

Trooper Blair
Newcastle Journal 5 December 1914

We went straight into one action after another without a rest. Since I last wrote to you, I have had very good luck. One day we went up with our horses to bring the guns out of action. There were 12 drivers, one corporal and a quartermaster. Whilst we were proceeding towards our guns the Germans fired five shots, and blew up part of the road. When the firing ceased we went in a fast gallop, but the firing began again, and was straight at us. The first shot went over us, but the second one dropped and burst between my horses and the gun

-limber. I was only two yards behind, and was nearly choked with dust and smoked. (sic) A piece of shrapnel whizzed past my face. Fortunately we all got through without a scratch. We have not had a single casualty, and we consider that we shall get through anything now. The gunners, who saw it all, were amazed at our escape, for they expected we would all be blown up. Don't think I was not frightened, for I was. The first time we were coming out of action, we were trotting out with the guns when a shell dropped just behind my waggon. We dashed off at full stretch, just in time to see a house fall in front of us. I was just able to turn my horses off, else we would have been under the lot. It occurred after dark, and when the officers and gunners congratulated me and asked me how I escaped, I was too full to speak to them.

Driver A. Younger, 3rd Northumbrian Brigade, Royal Field Artillery
Newcastle Evening Journal 14 July 1915

Yesterday I had tea with some real English women, and Cis Kelsey, my cousin, was one. I found out where she was, and yesterday, in a downpour of rain, I had an hour's hard riding, landing back to my camp about 8.30 p.m. She is just splendid. Her life is filled to the brim, and where she is she comes across the worst cases, as it is the main place for first dressing. She told me of two cases, one a Sunderland boy, shot through the body. He was only eighteen, but kept saying he had done his bit. The other was a man who had gone to gather a few "spuds" and had got shot through the back. Both were North Country lads. As you say the horses do catch it, but they are wonderful and so wise. My horse is jet black and his name is Sweep. He knows me fine, as we are never parted. I am always on the pinch for him - pea meal, grain, and grass.

Bombardier Robert
Robertson, 1st Battery
Royal Field Artillery
Newcastle Evening
Chronicle 18 September
1915

Tending a wounded horse
at No.5 Veterinary Hospital
Abbeville
©Imperial War Museums
(Q 10471)

WINTER CONDITIONS

The first phase of the war came to an end in December 1914 when both a series of unsuccessful attacks and the increasingly difficult winter conditions convinced the commanders to delay further serious fighting until the spring. The soldiers, however, had to find a means of surviving the increasingly uncomfortable conditions. The Indian troops in particular suffered greatly from frostbite and exposure.

I am still alive and kicking and having a rough time. I am right in the middle of the fighting, and kept going night and day. The ground is now covered with snow, and will be obliged if you will send me my muffler, a pair of gloves, and a thick pair of socks. My boot soles are going, and I may have a difficulty in getting any more. Send me some cigarettes and matches, as we cannot get any here. I have just got a wash - the first I have had for a fortnight - and, to make matters worse, I have no soap left. I have never had my clothes off this month, and my shirt is nearly walking away.

Driver W. Bennett, 26th Brigade, Royal Field Artillery Ammunition Column
Morpeth Herald, Friday 4 December 1914

We had a terrible time in the trenches, but that was the fault of the weather more than the Germans. It rained practically for the whole three days, and we were soaked to the skin, and the last day we were sitting in pools of water all day. We were in the reserve trenches, and, if anything, they were worse than in the firing line. If you can imagine four of us drenched under the kitchen table for 24 hours you will have some idea of what we were like. You can imagine how we yearned for the relief party after three such days. I believe we had only one man shot, but a good many will feel the effect of the weather for a long time to come.

One of our platoons was washed out altogether. Their trench was near a river which overflowed, and washed away their rifles and all their belongings and the men had to swim for their lives. However it is all over for the time being, and we can breathe for a few days. What a relief it is to be away from the danger zone for a short time. In spite of everything I am feeling wonderfully fit. We have had a hot bath this morning, and if I can get my hair cut this afternoon I shall feel more comfortable. We were told that a mail bag caught fire on December 27 and all the letters were burned, so it is probable that some of mine were destroyed. I received your nice letter just as we were going up to the trenches, I could not read it then, as we were on the march. So I read it by candlelight in the trenches about 2 o'clock in the morning. The first thing we did when we returned was to have a good feed. I had a mutton chop and chips, and I did enjoy it.

Private Norman Bell (Hawthorne Street, Newcastle)
Newcastle Evening Chronicle 19 January 1915

I have been in France for nearly three months, and, like the rest, I have had about enough of it. It is not the fighting, but the discomfort which sickens everybody. It is nothing but incessant rain here, with mud everywhere. Our clothing is plastered with a thick coating of clay, and we have given up all efforts to get it off. The only way is to cut a foot or two off all round the bottom of your overcoat, which numerous ingenious Tommies do to avoid the fatigue of carrying a few unnecessary pounds of weight about.

In the way of grub, however, everything is excellent. We have bread and fresh meat daily, and sometimes even butter. There is also a weekly issue of rum and tobacco. We also receive newspapers and mails daily. Our mechanical transport is marvellous. Our company has four large motor waggons, which take us to and from work, which is a perfect Godsend, as, in addition to our equipment and arms, we have to carry picks and shovels. The part played by the R.E.'s in the war is practically that of non-combatants. We really do no fighting - only work, though our rifles and ammunition are always within reach. Our work, however, is attended with no little danger, as we often have to do it without cover. As a rule, however, the bulk of it is done at night. Even then we occasionally get one picked off, though up till now we have been particularly lucky. When we came out the strength of the company was 240 odd, and it is now just over 180. Still, the wastage is nothing like all due to casualties.

Besides making new trenches, sometimes we are in the fire trenches with the infantry, repairing them and patching them up generally. It is the going and returning from work where the greatest hardships are met with. Sometimes we have to go through nearly a mile of communication trenches up to our knees in thick clayey mud. In addition to the state of affairs under foot, the trench is so narrow that one is smothered in mud with rubbing against the walls. There is often no room for two to pass in the communication trenches, and one day, when we were going through them, we came across another party working. To allow us to pass they lay down on their stomachs, and we walked on their backs. No sooner were we past them, than we met a man crawling on his hands and knees with another wounded on his back. To let them pass we had to lay down in a foot of water. I mention this incident to give you an idea of what things are really like. Of course in the fire trenches there is room to move about, and, as a rule, they are cleaner, as there is not so much traffic. In case you do not know, I may mention that a communication trench is one from the fire trench to the safety zone in the rear.

Anonymous soldier, 1ˢᵗ Siege Company, Royal Anglesey Engineers
Newcastle Journal 21 January 1915

Flooded Communications Trench
©Imperial War Museums (Q 4462)

We have had a spell this last week, and have had a chance of getting donned up a bit. We have received shirts, socks, drawers, mits, mufflers and sweets, writing paper and all sorts of things from England. This is the first chance we have had to get pulled up a bit, and it has done us a world of good, as we had not had a change, or had boots or socks off, for months.

We are in a position where the Germans, at the nearest point, are only a matter of 80 yards from the infantry trenches, but our Battery is two miles behind. When we came into this position three weeks ago, on a Sunday night, at about 11 p.m., myself and another signaller had to run a telephone wire from the battery to the infantry trenches, about two miles away, through ploughed fields and barbed wire. It was raining and snowing, and we were being fired on by the

Royal Engineers taking drums of telephone wires along a duckboard path to the front
©Imperial War Museums (Q 6050)

Germans, but they could not see us very well, as it was very dark, and when we reached the trenches, 50 yards from the Germans, it was 5 o'clock next morning. We had to stop in the trenches for eight days and nights.

We can't use flags or the heliograph out here. It is all telephone work, and when the wire gets cut by a shell or a bullet, it is very difficult to find the break. Of course, this has got to be done, and we think nothing of it.

Signaller J. Clark, 58th Battery, letter dated 2 December 1914
Newcastle Evening Chronicle 2 February 1915

They (*a pair of socks*) are the things that we most need, because, going in and out of the trenches, through the communication trenches, we have to go up to our knees in water, and, of course we get our feet wet. Moreover, it has a favourite trick of freezing at night, and if we have wet feet you can realise we don't have a very comfortable night. So a change of socks is very highly appreciated, I can assure you. No doubt you would like to know who we are and what we are. We are a part of the Indian contingent. We arrived in England from India on September 24th, had 4 hours' leave to see our parents, and left for France on November 5th - 12 days in England after six years - and we arrived just in time to catch the terrible weather. We have about 300 left out of 1,100 that came home from India with us. The rest have either been killed, wounded, or sent home ill - the majority with frost-bitten feet. Oh! it was terrible for us coming from the tropics and coming straight here before we were acclimatised, straight amongst the snow. I am glad the worst is over. It proved our worst enemy - the weather.

Anonymous soldier
Morpeth Herald 26 February 1915

I've a little wet home in a trench,
Which the rainstorms continually drench;
   There's a dead crow (sic) close by
   With her hoofs toward the sky,
And she gives off a beautiful stench;
Underneath, in the place of a floor,
There's a mass of wet mud and some straw;
   And the "Jack Johnsons" tear
   Through the rain-sodden air
O'er my little wet home in the trench.
There are snipers who keep on the go,
So you must keep your "napper" down low;
   And there's star-shells at night
   Make a deuce of a light,
Which causes the language to flow;
Then the "bully" and biscuits we chew,
For it's days since we tackled a stew,
   But with shells dropping there,
   There's no place can compare
With my little wet home in the trench.

Corporal Grey, 5th Northumberland Fusiliers
Morpeth Herald 19 February 1915

THE SPRING OFFENSIVE

When serious fighting began again in March, much of it was centred round the town of Ypres. The heavy losses of the autumn were replaced by the men of Kitchener's New Army, who had been urgently recruited after Mons, and following a short period of training in Britain, were now sent to the front. There was fighting at Neuve Chapelle, Hill 60, and St. Julien. For many from the North East, their baptism of fire came at the Battle of St. Julien, when they found themselves in the front line within days of landing in France.

We landed at the base a month to-day, and after getting fully equipped we proceeded to the firing line. We set off in the dark to march seven or eight miles to the trenches. This is a most dangerous performance, as the enemy send up flarelights which light up the places all round, and then they fire at you with both rifles and Maxim guns. We lost several men with the snipers before we got safely in about four o'clock in the morning. Things were quiet for some time, except for a few volleys, which we get used to. Our artillery started to find the range of the enemy between nine and ten o'clock in the morning. We had then another period of quietness. During this time in our part of the trench the sniper caught one of our men through the head and blew out his brains. He fell at my feet, and I bandaged him up, but he died in about ten minutes. A very good start for me, but I had more to come. I had a fine baptism of fire. Well, about three o'clock our artillery again started shelling the German trenches, and the Germans retaliated. This was kept up for three solid hours. In the trench where I was the Germans were only about forty yards away in their trenches. The duel was terrific. Thousands of shells burst over us, until one, alas, burst right in front of us, and then one behind. The next I will never forget. It burst in our trench and blew away our parapet. The lad next to me had his legs blown off, and my rifle was blown to pieces in my hands. There were 25 of us in this particular part in which I was, and there are only six of us left to tell the tale. There were six wounded, and the rest killed. I had a time getting the killed and wounded out, as I was the only non-commissioned officer left. Our officer was also wounded in the hip. We got back to rest in a barn, after being relieved by the Welsh, when we had a ration of rum, and, mind, we needed it. I was a pitiful sight, as I had been four or five hours - it seemed like an age - up to the waist in water and "sludge" in the communicating trenches. We rested for four days and got rigged up again. I had lost all except what I stood up in.
Lance-Corp. Frank Brodie, Northumberland Fusiliers, letter dated Easter Sunday (April 4)
Morpeth Herald 16 April 1915

The weather here continues to be fine, for which the troops are duly thankful. No longer have they to stand in the trenches up to the knees in mud and water. It is true the ground here is full of springs. If one digs deeply, it is impossible to drain. As fast as one bales, water oozes back again. You will have read of the successful explosions of mines here and the assault on German trenches. We still hold these trenches. The night of the attack we were in billets, but had a good view of the flashing of the guns. Unless people have seen big explosions they cannot realise what an unbroken series of huge bursts, lasting several hours, means. Those who have been here since the beginning tell me such shows are infrequent. It is bound to be so, from an economic point of view, if from no other. We expended 14,000 shells during the bombardment of the German lines. I estimate the cost of one night's bombardment at £280,000. What wonder that such shows are rare! As I write the beastly things keep whizzing and banging. The uncertainty of it all is all very disconcerting. Five minutes ago I saw two "Johnsons" fall in Ypres. Imagine a beautiful summer's day - and English country Sunday - in the distance the roar of an express train. Gradually it gets louder and louder, until the thudding roars in one's ears. Then, gradually - and you unconsciously thank God - the roar diminishes. The express train, as it were, has passed over your head, leaving you for the moment safe and breathing freely. Then a dull bang-boom! You look over the parapet and see in the clear distance a dense black cloud slowly rising and curling round the cathedral spire, shining white from amongst a miniature forest. The express train has exploded. One hopes for no casualties, and that the next express train may also go over one's head and far away. You are still watching the thick black cloud slowly disappearing into the still summer day - it is gone. You are turning away when a thin blue cloud of smoke from the same place rises - a house on fire - and everything is peaceful, like a summer day. Two yards away a man is frying bacon on a dying charcoal brazier. It all seems so strange. It is always Sunday here - no movement of any kind, and yet death broods over everything.

Second Lieutenant H. A, Iung, Northumberland Fusiliers, letter dated 20 April
Evening Chronicle 26 May 1915

We were ordered to take a big hill, (*Hill 60*) where the Germans were entrenched, so we blew it up, and then charged along with another regiment. The fun started when we had held it for a while, as they counter charged us. Our company, along with C company, was holding the trench, and it was terrible. The big guns were busting in our faces, and it was awful, holding out for about twelve hours until we were relieved. I got my bayonet broken on my rifle, and I had three different rifles. When they were too hot to hold we just laid them down and took one from our mates, who were dead or wounded. I never saw sights like it in all my life….. When we were relieved the enemy were shelling the dugouts that we were in, and whatever the stuff may be that they had in their shells, it nearly nipped the eyes out of us. Some of the chaps had been out since the start of the war, and they said it was the worst they had come through. They said that Mons could not be classed with it. The General was down in the camp to-day, and gave us great praise for the way we held on.

Private John Proudfoot, 2nd Battalion Kings Owns Scottish Borderers (Dumfries)
Southern Reporter 29 April 1915

Just a line to say I am all right. We have been having a rest yesterday and so far to-day, but don't know when we will be sent off again. We had a bad time of it on Saturday; marched a long way by night and through a certain city which was being heavily shelled. It was terrible. We suffered our first casualties there. They were busy giving the Cathedral a firing, and we got a bit of it as we passed it. We came on a mile or two and lay in a field from about 12.30 to 2.30 a.m. in pouring rain. Then we got up and marched another mile or so, and lay down again in a field which was being shelled. Then at about 7.30 did an attack. We had a little rest at night and till mid-day on Monday, then another attack and got in with some kilties. Today we have had to dig ourselves in and are waiting further orders. The shells are bursting all around like anything, "Jack Johnsons," "whiz-bangs," "grunches," shrapnel, etc., etc. The "Jack Johnsons" do not do much harm unless they hit a man, but they are terrifying things to hear whizzing overhead. I picked up a pretty useful rifle and bayonet on Monday in our attack and had some shots at them. The way the Germans systematically shelled our stretcher bearers while taking wounded off the field was damnable. While they were doing this they were showing a white flag. We took no notice. We have lost a lot of men. This part seems to be "the" part of the front. I bet there is no Brigade that has had such a time as we have had in one week. I am having to act second in command of the Company, what's left of it. They fairly shell all the roads here. Going through that city was awful. It seemed as if there was a service on in the Cathedral as the windows were all lit. Actually it was on fire. The "Cloth Hall" must have been a wonderful building. I had to get rid of my blanket and sheet on Sunday owing to weight but still have my pack. Most of the others have had to throw that way too. It is very fine today, beautifully warm. We just sit in a trench and snooze, etc., as we daren't show our heads. The snipers are awful at the front. On Sunday every time my head went up a machine gun was turned on and the bullets whizzed past. On Monday too the rifles were busy. They seem to get close up.

Ruins of the Cathedral and Cloth Hall Ypres
©Imperial War Museums (E (AUS) 1122)

I have nothing but praise for the Berwick lads. The way they faced the music was wonderful. You would thing it was their ordinary daily work.

F. B. Cowen, Lieutenant, 7th Northumberland Fusiliers
Berwick Advertiser 7 May 1915

We are away from the firing line now, after having had eight days of it, and, to tell the truth, I am not sorry. We left it in the early hours of Monday, and marched practically till last night, with only a few hours' rest. We are in a rest-camp for a week or so, till we pull ourselves together again.

Our brigade suffered heavily, but the casualties are principally wounded. We were right in the thick of everything, and it was awful. Old soldiers said that there had never been anything to equal the artillery duel in any previous war. I have had several narrow escapes. One was when a shrapnel shell burst close to where five of us were in a trench. It blew us all out of it. It is not the shells that worry me most, but their snipers, who have a "pop" at one every now and then. I have a slight scar on one of my fingers where one of their bullets slid across my hand. We had an hour's heavy shelling on the Sunday night before we left the trenches, but we just sat tight and came through all right.

We had a big inspection yesterday morning by Sir John French, who praised our brigade and made sympathetic references to General Riddell and Captain Nash. Captain Nash, by the way, was the only one killed in our company. The saddest sight of all was when he was buried by moonlight the next night. The whole company presented arms as the body passed down the lines.

General French said he was obliged to send us straight to the firing line. But we had done what no other brigade had done, by going straight there and passing through such an ordeal successfully. Not one of us knows yet what we went through when we made the advance a week past Monday. We advanced from trench to trench under a perfect hail of rifle fire, maxim fire and shrapnel, and, by drawing the fire of the Germans from the Canadians and Indians, we enabled them to advance and capture one or two most vital points.

Private Ted Shilan, 5th Northumberland Fusiliers
Newcastle Evening Chronicle 12 May 1915

On Sunday night we started on our first engagement. We advanced across a field in extended order under our artillery fire, and when we had advanced about half a mile the Germans, who had got our range, began shelling us. The shells came from all directions, and the wonder is that there were not more casualties. About an hour after we were told to retire. I think we were there to draw the enemy's artillery fire from some other position, so that another regiment had little to do but to walk in and take the position. At any rate, we got out of it with only one officer killed and two men wounded. After that we slept in a field a mile or two behind, and the next morning we had again to dig ourselves in. When daylight broke the Germans once more shelled us, and we had to be pretty smart to get our trenches dug in time. We stayed in them a week.

All the farms round about were shelled and burned down. There was a battery close by, which was also shelled, and two men and three horses were killed. Here we stayed, living mainly on bully beef and biscuits. We had very little tea, as we were unable to light a fire, because of the aeroplanes flying about - probably locating our positions. We had the satisfaction of bringing down a German aeroplane one day. The pilot was dead when he reached the ground, and the observer died shortly after of wounds. Both seemed to be hardly 20 years old. The first few days we were doing nothing but eating and sleeping, but the last few nights we were out all night digging trenches. It was not a pleasant experience digging in the dark. The Germans have a very good device for seeing in the dark. They send up a rocket, and when it gets over our lines it bursts into flames just like electric lights. When there are a few dozen of them they light up the place for a good distance. As soon as the flame shows itself there comes a shower of bullets.

On May 2 we were told that we were to go to a rest camp; and the news was received with joy all round. When we started there was the same process to go through as when we went into the firing line. We marched about six miles to some huts, where we stayed for the night. It was on that march that we lost those seven men killed by one shell. Another march of 12 miles was followed by being billeted in some farms - in the hay-lofts or wherever room could be found. On May 4 we were inspected by General French, who complimented us highly upon the way in which we had gone into action. He added that if we were needed again he hoped we would respond in the same way. We would not have been in the firing line so soon had it not been for the French retreating that week-end. We have been billeted in a pretty country village where the scenery is the best we have seen so far. The weather is so summer-like that at night we take our blankets and topcoats and sleep outside. The only things cheap out here are eggs. You can buy them a penny each (boiled if you like). We are having a canny life here.

Private George Sowerby, 9th Durham Light Infantry
Newcastle Evening Chronicle 21 May 1915

British reserve troops entering the billet in a farm house behind the firing line

A SOLDIER'S LOT

In a Belgian village, I was billeted in a small house, in which there was a scarcity of beds. When time for going to bed came, I heard a rustling in the corner of the room; you may imagine my feelings when I discovered the cause. It was an old woman, who had been confined to bed for many years, ordering her daughter to lift her over so that her bed might be given to the soldier. I thanked her very much, and slept on the floor.

An anonymous Eyemouth soldier
Berwick Advertiser 12 March 1915

Well, mother, I suppose you will be very pleased to know that I have won the D.C.M. I had better not tell you what I did, or you may think that I have gone of my "nut." But you have not to be afraid of anything out here. I never experienced anything like the fighting on Whit Monday. The Germans started at 2 a.m., and they never stopped till Tuesday night, sending their gas bombs in galore. Men were dying 'on piece.'
To tell you the truth, I could sit down and have a good cry at the thought of these poor men. And people in England can now think of going on strike! I don't know what to make of them. Men out here are working day and night for a shilling. I don't know what would become of England if we were to go on strike. It breaks the hearts of soldiers who left good jobs to come out here.

Private A. P. Stokes DCM, 5th Battalion Northumberland Fusiliers
Newcastle Journal 1 June 1915

At night we sometimes went trench-digging, or carrying barbed wire and other things to the engineers. One night we went in front of our firing line with poles and barbed wire. It was the first experience of being in the firing line. The bullets were flying in all directions, and those lights were going up in dozens. We soon got used to them after we had been there a day or two. We remained in those trenches for six days, and were shelled every day. Whilst there our rations were very good, and as we were allowed to make fires, we got a lot of cooked stuff, made by ourselves, of course.
Drinking water was very scarce, but we got over that difficulty, as we dug deep holes by the side of the trenches and in the morning there was generally plenty of water, only it needed boiling. So we lighted fires during the day, and made ourselves tea and cocoa. Also we got bacon for breakfast, which we cooked. We were here five days when the Royal Fusiliers relieved us. We arrived in a wood six miles behind the firing line feeling a little tired. Owing to the weakened force

of our platoon we got very little sleep in the trenches, as we were constantly on sentry duty. On Sunday we had a novelty - an open-air service was held behind the wood. One night there was an "al fresco" concert in a field. The band of the R.A.M.C. rendered selections, and we spent a very enjoyable evening. There were all sorts or soldiers from different regiments, and there was no lack of artists.

George E. Sowerby, 9th Durham Light Infantry
Newcastle Journal 12 June 1915

We are staying in huts, which are all right so long as the Germans keep the shells away. We deserve a good rest after being in the firing line for 16 days. When we were sent up, we went to reinforce the Royal Scots, and a fine set of chaps they are. We had to march through a town which is an absolute ruin. It was on fire, and we had to run through the streets with fire on each side. Then we started to get the shells, and later we got amongst rifle fire. Bullets were whizzing all over, but we were lucky and got through without anyone being hit. We gave the Germans some of "Tickler's artillery," as the Scottish boys term it. They are bombs in the shape of Tickler's jam tins. Being only a few yards from their trenches we were able to throw them. Of course practised men do it. Then we went into some dug-outs, and there we had our jolliest lad knocked out. The bullets were always flying about and one got him.

Private I Pearce, 5th Durham Light Infantry
Newcastle Evening Chronicle 3 June 1915

Making hand grenades out of tins

We have had some awful times, but I would not like to have been on the German side. On Wednesday morning they got a smashing up. Our artillery rained shells into them, and our men charged over 300 yards of ground and got their trenches, killing hundreds. After a few minutes we got their second and third lines and took about 900 prisoners. I saw a good many of them and they were a very poor set, clothes all worn, and shabby boots. I was on guard at the time, and could see the firing line plainly. What an awful sight it was! It was impossible for any man to live under such shell fire. Our wounded came back carrying German helmets, swords, caps, and all smiling after the charge. I saw some of the 7th D.L.I., shot through the arm, and gave them a drink of water as they were going to the hospital. If we had lost many men, there were thousands to take their place, but the wounded said the firing line was crowded, and not room for one more man. We had only about 19 killed, but a good many wounded. The Germans asked who let the British out of Hell. A place that we pass is named Hell Corner, and it is well named, for the shells do fly past. But the Germans have found their match. If we are ordered to take trenches, we do it, and the Germans cannot stop us. They have good artillery, but their infantry is not worth twopence a box. They are dead frightened of our artillery, and will not face our infantry. As soon as they see the bayonet, they are off.

Lance-Corporal W. Chapman, 9th Battalion Durham Light Infantry
Newcastle Evening Chronicle 27 June 1915

How would you like to receive your letters at daybreak? That is the time we get ours. It is comical to see everyone of us trying to read them. The light is not too good at that time 2.30. After it gets brighter out come the letters again, and we find that sometimes we have missed the best part of them. For the past week we have been in the worst part of the line. Only 12 yards between ours and the Huns trenches in one part of the line. On Wednesday last while another part of the line was attacking, we had to open out with rapid fire so as to keep the Germans from sending reinforcements from our part to where the attack was made. We had an hour and ten minutes at rapid fire, and while it lasted it was good sport, but we paid for it in the afternoon and night. The Huns shelling our trenches most successfully. One Jack Johnson landed on top of our trench, and I got buried, but got out again. Seven of our fellows were wounded with that shell, two seriously, as you can see our lot out here is not a happy one.
One incident in the attack that day is worth telling. While the Highlanders were charging with the bayonet, one of them saw two Germans retiring with a Maxim gun. He threw down his rifle, ran after them, knocked them down with his fist, took the Maxim off them, and then turned the gun on all the Huns who

were retiring. I think that is a good case of adding insult to injury.

Corporal George McLeod, 7th Battalion Northumberland Fusiliers
Newcastle Evening Chronicle 27 June 1915

I am still keeping "in the pink." I am writing this in the trenches. We have been four days in the firing line, and it is very quiet here compared with what we have been used too. (sic) A few shells and rifle bullets sail over our heads to let us know they are as much awake as we are. You will be surprised to know we are having new potatoes in the trenches. They are growing between the lines, and we made up our minds to have some. We managed to get as many as made a dinner, but were glad to get back, for the German snipers were on our track.

Private James Gould, 4th Battalion, Northumberland Fusiliers
Newcastle Evening Chronicle 8 July 1915

We are running a field hospital for the care of the sick and wounded. We are still within shell range, however, and we get a few shells over almost every day. The Germans are not particular where they put their shells, and they have managed to hit 4 women coming along the road since coming here, but they were only slightly hurt. Our dressing station proved very handy, for the poor women were taken in, and their injuries dressed. Our lads have had to dig two graves here by the roadside in order to bury 2 soldiers (infantry) who had died of wounds after having been brought into our place. They were wrapped in blankets tied with tape, and a wooden cross marks the spot. At present the rain is pouring down, and it needs all our efforts to keep the water out of our bivouacs. Goodness knows when the war will end. By the way, we have sports very often, just a mile behind the firing line, and its good fun to witness the tussles between the Canadians and N.F.'s. Talk about nerve-racking! We are just a few hundred yards from a battery of guns, and when they get going we have to keep hold on our hats. We were just nicely interested in a wrestling match the other night when the Huns started their "sport," and the Canadians shouted to them to stop until the match was finished. However, a Durham county man beat the Canadian by 2 holds to one. To finish the good night's entertainment, the winner gave us a treat at weight-lifting.

Private W. Anderson, Royal Army Medical Corps
Newcastle Evening Chronicle 13 July 1915

Last night our ration party had a stormy time. Just as the party was coming up our artillery opened fire on the German trenches. The Germans replied very hotly, and the party had to leave more than half of our rations, which are now lost to us, worse luck. Last night's bombardment started about eleven o'clock and lasted for an hour and a quarter. Our artillery, 72 big guns, opened fire all together on a big fort or redoubt, just in front of my particular trench. You can fancy what it was like. But when nearly a hundred German guns are added, every one hurling as many shells as could be hurled, without melting the gun, I think your imagination will not be strong enough to enable you to conjure up what the row and slaughter was like. Our guns don't behave like that very often, but I can honestly say, when they do start, they can hit the mark, and they don't waste much. Looking over our trench now and again I could see the German trench and parapet flying all over the shop. The whole affair, apart from the danger, was the most fascinating spectacle I have ever witnessed. Shell fire simply mows the men down. They don't even get a fighting chance. I have not had a hot meal since I came out to these trenches, because, as sure as we light a fire, Fritz (we call the Germans Fritz) will put a shell over and spoil our meal for us. We have tried it once or twice, and he has knocked soil all over us and our food. There is only one thing I don't like about him. He very seldom puts his head up. But I have caught him several times during this last few weeks. The best day I have had was on June 19, when I got six out of two parties who were working at the back of their trenches. As you know quite well, at such a distance I never miss. Just fancy our being 25 yards apart, and my missing them! The first one I miss I will let you know of it, and then you can burn that shooting medal of mine. I do nothing all day but lie waiting for Fritz to show his head. When he does, I make him bite lumps out of the sandbags. The dirty blackguards! Yesterday, in addition to losing nearly all our rations, a lump of shell struck my pack and haversack. It cut the straps of both, through the tin you sent me, in which I had fags and matches. It struck the matches, spoiled half of my fags, and passed out of the bottom of my pack. I don't care how often it hits my pack, so long as it does not hit me, as I don't fancy being hit by shrapnel. But if my turn comes I shall take it without grumbling. As the trenches we are in belonged to the Germans at one time, they have the range too fine, and that is one thing I don't like.

Sergeant J. Furness, 10th Battalion Durham Light Infantry
Newcastle Evening Chronicle 17 July 1915

I have been only ten yards off the German sappers; they work at night underground, to try and lay a mine under our trench, and if we can discover the sapping so much the better. Only yesterday they managed their work, but I am pleased to say that our men were not in the trench; the listening post brought the warning in time. We are doing exactly the same work, and whoever gets there first scores. We scored a hit yesterday. We got into the sap without them knowing, and our sappers just packed the explosives under and blew them up. We did not know how many Germans were working, and less did we care. They got a few tons of earth over them, so there was no need for a burial service.

Private H. Taylor, 6th Battalion Durham Light Infantry
Newcastle Evening Chronicle 22 July 1915

We, as engineers, are putting up wire entanglements in front of our own trenches. When we want to advance, we have to go out and cut the entanglements down. This work is done lying on one's back - not a very comfortable position. Of course, it is done at night. Where we are camping the Huns send shells over almost daily, but they don't do much damage. Here are a few names of the trenches - York House, the Fosse, Stink Cottage, Piccadilly, Watling Street, and Regent Street.

Wiring Party at work at Night
©Imperial War Museums (Q 6419)

A lot of the lads out here know that I am a North-Eastern League referee, and also a League Linesman, and they are great supporters of local teams. Besides, some of them play the game themselves, and they mostly belong to Tyneside. We all want to know if you think you could get us a football. It would be very welcome in our spare time out of the trenches, and would also remind us of the old times at home, especially on Tyneside, where they followed the game very closely.

Sapper Joseph Ayres, 2/1 Field Company, Northern Division, Royal Engineers
Newcastle Evening Chronicle 23 August 1915

We have moved again and pitched our tents elsewhere. We set away at 8.30 p.m. with full kit on. It is quite true what a man said about the British soldier - "a man that walks along with a lot of things hung on him." We were like a set of pedlars. To make matters worse it rained and the wind blew, and was pitch dark. About 10.30 we passed through a big town, marching through the streets with never a song or a whistle, the tramp of our feet and the rattle of the transports being enough to waken the dead. Now and then we could see an upstairs shutter open and some French mademoiselle peep out to see what was passing, but it was only a sight which is common to them now - "Soldats Anglais." We also passed some big casualty hospitals, and even in the dark one could see the handsome type of buildings. Soon we were out of the town on the roads again which go in a straight line for miles, having a row of tall trees along each side. The road-surface is the best thing ever been created to torture anyone who has to tramp along it. In the middle it is badly paved with square cobbles, about three yards wide, whilst at each side is about three yards of mud. Now picture to yourself this tramp. It was pitch dark, and one was just able to discern the man in front. We skirted along the road in this fashion some two to three miles behind the firing line. The German star shells lighted everything up brilliantly for a while, and then all was again pitch dark, and we floundered about until another came. Added to this was the rifle and Maxim fire and the pouring rain, whilst at intervals Red Cross cars would come along and push us off the road. We would enter a small place and a voice would come out of the darkness. "Is that the Seconds?" "Aye, hinney" we would shout back. Then the voice bids us follow him, and we get taken in tow for about another ten minutes, when we reach a small farm, where two small barns are prepared to receive nearly 300 men. We get into them at 1.30 a.m. after a tramp of thirteen miles in the wind and rain. We off with our sheets, packs, boots, and puttees, and loosed our great coats, wrapped ourselves up, lay down and were soon asleep. Could a photo be taken of the inside of these small barns it would form a sight - heads all round, feet in the middle, a lot of heads, feet and bodies in the middle, sleeping the sleep of the just, tired out.

Private William Barrett, B Section Royal Artillery
Newcastle Evening Chronicle 11 August 1915

I have had about an hour of the most intense excitement I ever experienced. My pal and I were cooking our breakfast when all the German inventions seemed to intrude our feast. I had my mouth full of bacon and bread when a shell exploded somewhere near me. We did not know where to turn to dodge them. I took my canteen lid off the fire with the bacon in it, and also what was left of the tea. I tried to work my way back to the dug-out, but a piece of shell sent my canteen lid flying across the trench. I went after it, and behold my bacon was still there, but, alas, my gravy was all gone. We did not know which dug-out was going up next, and here I am writing this with not a tab for breakfast. No one has been hit, and no dug-out struck, so here we are, all that's left of the Tyneside Terriers...... I shot a hare one night, and you should have seen me cleaning it. But, oh, the cooking! I looked round for a bucket, but could find nothing but a biscuit tin. We managed to have a tasty feed. I will have to close, for the shells are coming again, and we have a man to bury who was shot through the head.

Pioneer James Brown, 5th Battalion Northumberland Fusiliers
Newcastle Evening Chronicle 25 August 1915

Through the massive portals of a gateway we marched with weary limbs, and lay down to rest, some of us in large wooden sheds, some in the rooms of a deserted mansion, and a few others, of whom I was one, in a small vinery. It was turned midnight when we arrived. The small all-night lightness of the sky was sufficient to guide us to our various billets. With reveille it was as if we had been translated into another world. After a long spell in the trenches, with a tropical sun often beaten down on our heads or half--drenched with the thunder rain, the shelter and shade of magnificent trees and the odour of many flowers were indeed refreshing to our tired bodies and strained nerves, for we awoke to find ourselves in a veritable paradise. Here a long wide border was set apart for rose-bushes, all now in full bloom, delicate in shade, rich in scent; there a large bed of begonias offered a contrast to the rose garden, for the colouring, though as varied, was deep and bright. In a secluded part of the grounds, sheltered by overhanging trees, principally acacias and chestnut, and surrounded by flowering shrubs, lay, invitingly cool, a deep pond. It was indeed to be "beside the still waters," to lie on the green sward near and live over again the many happy days spent in similar surroundings in England. In the cool of the evening, after the parades of the day were over, I had a walk along the banks of the slow-moving river, a field's length away from our billet. It was practically the first moving water I had seen since landing in France, and certainly the only stream of any size. Here I found myself in my element - a botanist's paradise of wild flowers. Willow herb, meadow-sweet, tansy, and purple loose-strife were growing in great profusion, whilst such flowers as the yellow water-lily, water plantain and arrow-head brightened up the margin of the stream. ...In the west the sun is setting, throwing into relief the outlines of a distant village and innumerable trees, and making the river appear like a stream of gold. So I return with many a "bon soir" to elderly Frenchmen or pretty girls taking their evening stroll. They return the salute, and seem pleased at the recognition given. The days are growing shorter, and by nine o'clock the moon has risen, outlining, as it were in silver, hundreds of small fleecy clouds. A perfect summer night - a night to sit in the open and build castles in the air. We squat about here and there, most of us thinking of home, a word which has an added meaning for us all. Sometimes in such moments we think of other homes - homes in which there is silence and sorrow, homes made desolate by the loss of loved ones in the field, and often our eyes become strangely moist when we remember how such and such a comrade died. But though they are gone from our ranks, their presence is still felt amongst us, and we are all the better soldiers for the sacrifice they have made.

In the courtyard a Tommy is reciting "Gunga Din" to an admiring and attentive crowd. The officers leave their after-supper talk to listen to him and say to one another "Capital, isn't he!" And so think we all, for our elocutionist comrade is a great asset to the company, and many a happy hour is spent listening to his recitals. He finishes, there is a pause; then, as the applause dies away, the crowd disperses, for it is time to "get down to it," and soon we are all wrapped in blanket and great coat, and in the land of dreams.

Lance-Corporal R. H. Temple, 4th Battalion Northumberland Fusiliers
Newcastle Evening Chronicle 27 August 1915

We are engaged preparing our winter quarters, which is giving us a good deal of extra work at the moment. But we shall have the benefit of it later as the rain comes through the dug-outs like blazes. A chap here in the trenches wrote a series of songs, and we have two "sing-songs" in a farmhouse near our position twice a week. We were entertained last night by the "Bombers' Band," of the 5th N.F., who are holding our trenches. The "band" is made up of one big drum (a biscuit-tin), two side-drums (jam-tins), five combs covered with paper, and two mouth-organs. One of the chaps has a melodeon, and I can tell you he gets some stuff out of it. This is how we keep alive in our spare moments. If it were not for these outbursts we should come badly on. As far as possible, we try to forget our position and where we are.

Anonymous Gunner, Northumbrian Division, Royal Field Artillery
Newcastle Evening Chronicle 30 August 1915

There are three of us and one Lance-Corporal on a sniping and observation post in an old farm house, about 700 yards behind the firing line. And, my word, what a hot spot it is! We started on this post Sunday morning. Well, in the afternoon the Germans shelled us out, and we had to retire into a small dug-out in the rear of the farm. The Germans slung some shells right into the building, but I am pleased to say no one was hit, barring a smothering with dust and bricks. You see they gave us no warning. The first shell burst about 15 feet from us, and just in front of the building. Of course we cleared out immediately, but shells were falling thick and fast. We waited about half-an-hour, and then returned to our post inside the house. Luck seemed to favour us, for we weren't molested any more that day. We returned to this post before day-break this morning, and had just got settled down to take observation when, whiz-bang! and a shell dropped right into the rear of the building. Of course, we collared our rifles and telescopes, and scooted for the dug-out, but just as we were going out of what was once the back door another shell fell not three yards away. I was behind the wall, but how the two chaps who were behind me escaped being hit I don't know, God must have been between them and the shell. The force of the explosion sent a bucket filled with water flying over, and one of the chaps (a B Company man) was crouching beside it. Well, they only gave us three that time. We stayed in the dug-out half-an-hour, and then returned to our post, but we hadn't been there a quarter of an hour before they started shelling us again. Another rush for the dug-out, with shrapnel and bricks flying around us. We were hit ever so many times with very small pieces of shell and bricks, but again nobody was hurt, excepting my pal of B Company, who got a smack in the side with a brick, which made a bruise, but that was all. The Germans sent four over this time.

You can imagine we were a bit shaky after that, the whole four of us; so we stayed in the dug-out about an hour, and then for the third time this morning, we resumed observations at our post again, feeling anything but safe. However, we weren't bothered with any more shells after that, and to get our own back, managed to plug two Germans at a range of 900 yards. It is really very exciting, for we see any number of Germans, whereas the men in the trenches seldom see one from one month's end to another.

Private Frank F. Young, B Company, 9th Battalion Northumberland Fusiliers
Newcastle Evening Chronicle 5 October 1915

GAS ATTACKS

The Germans first used poison gas at the Second Battle of Ypres on 22 April 1915. By September of that year, the British were also using it as a weapon. The following accounts describe its impact on the soldiers.

.... the Germans are setting fire to everything they can - towns and hospitals and they are firing liquid shells into the trenches. The stuff that comes off them blinds you for a good while and then you start to cough, your eyes run "like bairns crying going to school on Monday morning!" Your eyes get red as blood and you can't stand the pain.

Private Robert Cockburn, 2nd Battalion, King's Own Scottish Borderers
Berwick Advertiser 7 May 1915

We doubled through a big town one night when the houses around us were falling like skittles, where we saw the real devastation of war. Teams of horses lay where they had fallen, and here and there human bodies, civilians amongst them. Such sights as these gave us perhaps an idea of what the state of things would be like as we approached nearer the trenches. For myself. I don't seem

Gas Attack at the opening of the Battle of Loos
©Imperial War Museums (HU 63277B)

to remember much about our advance, except a queer sensation. First, my eyes began to smart and water, and I felt altogether funny. We had been "gassed" by yellow fumes from shells that had burst like ordinary shells amongst us. When carrying our first patient out of fire we took cover with the stretcher in a ditch, and applied water and handkerchiefs to our mouths, which somewhat prevented further "gassing."

Bandsman W. Bonner, a stretcher bearer with the Northumbrian Division
Newcastle Journal 18 May 1915

You will no doubt have read about the enemy using poisonous gas upon us, but, thank God, we are better prepared for it now, as we have all been served with respirators, to combat with it. I am pleased to say that in many cases the wind has changed round and carried the gas back to their own trenches. We exploded a lovely mine on Sunday morning, which our men had dug underground from our trench to theirs, and sent about 70 feet of their trench up into the air, together with arms, legs, bodies, sandbags and earth. It was lovely to see it, and, of course, our men were all waiting in our trenches for any who tried to get away. At the same time, our artillery gave them a most severe pounding, blowing the remainder of their trenches to pieces. Hurry up and get out; we can do with you.

Private A. E. Quincey, 2nd Battalion Durham Light Infantry writing on 13 May.
Newcastle Evening Chronicle 19 May 1915

I have had a very near shave of going to kingdom come with gas which the "baby-killers" send over. It is, I can assure you, worse than being wounded or even killed, as the agony is terrible. It knocks one straight out without showing blood, and causes one's throat to feel as though a red-hot poker had been put down. a man is very lucky if he gets over it, so I must be one of them I have turned nearly stone-blind in my right eye, and may get sent over to England for an operation.

Private D. Moor 2nd Battalion Royal Inniskilling Fusiliers
Newcastle Evening Chronicle 19 May 1915

..... You will have read about the Germans using gas. The German trenches were 150 yards away, when three other lads and myself went on to listening patrol. We were within 50 yards of the trenches, when I saw great green clouds coming from them, so we ran back to warn our fellows.
We got our respirators on, but some of our lads got it badly. I got only a whiff. It travels for miles, and turns everything made of brass or metal into a green colour. It was a good job they did not advance behind it, else they would have

got it hot. We were ready for them our artillery got going, and blew them and their trenches to bits. A German officer and sergeant came over to our trenches, and had the cheek to ask them to surrender. The answer was a few bits of lead. The officer had an iron cross and an old mouth organ out of tune.

Private I. Pearce, 5th Durham Light Infantry
Newcastle Evening Chronicle 3 June 1915

After our four days' rest (*18-21 May*) we again left for the trenches, and reached the reserve lot. We were there for a couple of days, and then took the first line, being relieved by the 7th Durhams. Just as it was breaking day over came a cloud of that poisonous gas, and soon it had us all spitting and coughing. It got into our eyes and nearly blinded us. I thought it was all over with us. You should have seen the colour of our bayonets when it was over - all black, as were the rings on the men's fingers.

After it had cleared, the Huns made an advance, and soon we had the satisfaction of popping bullets into them. The Germans advanced in thousands, and then our machine guns began to play upon them, and what with that and rapid rifle and artillery fire we played havoc with them. Soon they had to retire, leaving behind them hundreds of dead, also about 300 prisoners. After having ceased fire the roll was called, and in our platoon it was found that there were only 20 men left out of 48. The rest had been taken to the hospital, "gassed." Other platoons had suffered the same way.

George E. Sowerby, 9th Durham Light Infantry
Newcastle Journal 12 June 1915

It was about 6 o'clock on Whit Sunday night that word came for the 8th Durhams to fall in...We got up quite safe to our appointed place, where half the battalion was left in dug-outs in a wood, while the other half was put into a trench. All went well until 2 o'clock on Monday morning, when one of the lads on the look-out said gas was coming over from the left. We all made a dive for our respirators, and got them on just in time. Shells came bursting overhead with gas, just like a huge green wave coming to the ground. It went sweeping onward to the wood, where it caught our poor lads sleeping, and many of them will never awake again in this world - gassed before help could get over to them. For hours we were shown what Germany used to her enemies. Word was then brought round to take off our respirators. What a sight it was as we looked into each other's faces! It was one that will never fade from our memories. Shell after shell dropped among us, killing many of our men.

Private E. Tendall, 8th Battalion Durham Light Infantry
Newcastle Evening Chronicle 12 June 1915

I was "gassed" at Ypres on May 12 while performing my duty with a water party. After obtaining the water I despatched my men one by one, as, you know, if we had all attempted to return to the trenches together, and a shell had come over and caught us, we would have all; gone to meet our Maker. I was the last to leave, and as I was in the act of retracing my steps to the trenches I heard a shell coming over, so I immediately got down on my stomach, and, believing it had passed over our quarter, I raised my head, with the result that I had the misfortune to get the full contents of the gas from the shell into my face. When I became aware that I had been "gassed" I instantly turned into the road that lead back to the chateau, where we drew the water, and, being in possession of some salt, I prepared an emetic which warded off the more serious effects of the gas. I was in Le Harve (sic) Hospital a while, and I am very thankful that I am getting all right again.

Lance Sergeant F. Dodd, Durham Light Infantry
Newcastle Evening Chronicle 16 July 1915

The Germans have very cruel methods. Their shells when they burst give rise to fumes which very soon send us to sleep. When they get tired of shelling us they send gas over; it is very severe for the eyes and breathing. I have sampled, it, and I think it is a cruel way of killing men. I am glad to see our great wise men at home are getting more enlightened as to the ways and means to use for our soldiers safety. The Germans are trying their utmost to win, and are using cruel methods; and the only way for to win is to scheme to kill as they do. If some people at home had a bit of the gas that we get, it would broaden their views. There is not much merriment in warfare, unless you get the Germans on the run, and we feel happy in the thought that we are driving the enemy away from the homes we love in dear old England.

Private H. Taylor, 6th Durham Light Infantry
Newcastle Evening Chronicle 22 July 1915

THE BATTLE OF HOOGE

Hooge was another of the villages around Ypres. On 30 July 1915, the Germans launched a counter attack there, for the first time using flame throwers.

We are in the biggest fighting district in the line. Before the big battle we were in the trenches 15 days at -----, and one night we marched to -----. We had been there two days when the order came for us to get into fighting order. That meant no pack, just water-bottle, haversack and a few biscuits. We were then marched into a town hall for a lecture from the General Officer commanding the division who started like this; "Well, officers, N.C.O.'s and men of the 2nd D.L.I., I have come to let you know that the division has been picked to take the last trenches at Hooge; not only that, but that regiment has been picked to lead the advance." Our hearts began to get hot, at least mine did, when he said that "it was a tough job, and that the only thing to do was for every man to do his bit." You will know by now that every man in the Durhams did his bit. We set off for the march to Hooge, but the Germans had got wind of it, and when we were going up the road they shelled us, wounding 31 and killing 9. We still kept on and landed in the trenches at eleven o'clock at night and for the next two days we were viewing their great position, thinking how awful it would be to take barbed wire hundreds of yards deep. We knew it had to be done, and at half-past two in the morning of the 9th we were led into a wood and got orders to lie down; and then hell opened. Our artillery opened fire, and they replied. It was simply awful; but we lay there waiting for the order to charge. It came, and we went like mad, fighting hand-to-hand, and bayoneting the bounds. I did not like to kill, but I did it, and wanted more. We got into the first line, and went straight on to the fourth, and past it, and then dug ourselves in under hell's flames - nothing less. You will hardly credit what I did. I sat down and lit a cigarette for the simple reason that I was not in my right senses. I stuck there by myself for 16 hours, and all the time there was heavy bombardment. I was expecting every minute to go to glory, but I still kept on smoking. When night came on I got out and went back. When we were all formed up we got anything we wanted. I know I got a gill of rum and went to sleep. When we woke up we were marched back to rest, where we are now; and it was well earned. We are nearly ready to go back again.

A Private, 2nd Battalion Durham Light Infantry
Newcastle Evening Chronicle 14 September 1915

I was in the battle at Hooge. We were the attacking battalion, and were in the centre. It was an easy job taking the position we were ordered to take, and we succeeded with very little resistance and very few casualties through the good marksmanship of our artillery. But when we started to dig ourselves in the Germans bombarded us from all directions. Before we started we were told what would happen. Our bomb-throwers and all the officers and men took no notice of the shells that were bursting all around us. There were all sorts of shells, from "Jack Johnsons" to the ordinary hand bomb. The Germans have a bomb called the aerial torpedo. You can see it coming through the air, and can tell where it is going to drop, so you can make off in a different direction from that in which it is going; but in the circumstances we had to take our chance. A lot of our chaps saw death coming, but they stuck to their posts. There were some queer sights to be seen. We built our front up, just to be knocked down, and we were kept busy in this manner all day long. I was in a traverse, and was shifted to another. I left a couple of German helmets in the former, and when I went back for them the traverse was all smashed in. Some of our chaps had been buried, and were digging themselves out. I said to myself "It was lucky that I was shifted." I never looked again for the souvenirs, and though "If I get out of this scrape, I will be the best souvenir to bring home." Our battalion should have been relieved the same night, but we were cut off from all communication. We got relieved just as they could get at us.

Private Henry Cowen, 2nd Battalion Durham Light Infantry
Newcastle Evening Chronicle 25 August 1915

You will have read about the trenches we took back. Early in the morning we filed out of the trenches into the open at the edge of a wood and lay down in formation ready for the attack. About 2.15 our artillery started the bombardment, and the Germans opened fire. This did not last long, but just before our artillery ceased firing, we got the order to advance. Everybody was up, and made straight for the trenches. I think it was one of the biggest surprises the Germans ever had, because we were in possession before they knew where they were. Our artillery played their part well, and the trench was soon full of dead and wounded Germans. Even those who did not take part in the fight came over and gave themselves up as prisoners. We took more trenches than we were supposed to take. The Germans retired all along the line. Afterwards we worked like slaves to get the parapets of the trenches reversed so as to get a bit of cover for ourselves, for the Germans had opened heavy fire on us. It was terrible, and the ground shook in fearful fashion. We were losing men, and I was hit on the head by shrapnel, but I did not leave the firing line. My comrade put a bandage on, and I was still there, if anything else happened. Every rifle that leaves the firing line makes a lot of difference. I stuck to my souvenir - a German officer's revolver, which I took from him. It was a beauty. After five hours I thought I would make my way to the dressing station. This was a bit of a nerve-tickler, as we had to come down a communication trench, which the Germans were shelling severely. It was half-closed when I ventured through, but I managed it all right. I sat down for a rest, when I was hit again by a bursting shell. I got a nasty bruise on the leg, and had my hand hit. My rifle was splintered to bits. As soon as the shelling cooled down, I proceeded on my journey to the dressing station.

Lance Corporal Shotton, 2nd Battalion Durham Light Infantry
Newcastle Evening Chronicle 25 August 1915

We were out of the trenches for a few days' rest, but on the second morning our rest was broken by the Germans. There was a very heavy bombardment, which started about 2 o'clock in the morning. It awoke all the camps for miles around and we were ordered to "stand to" about 2.30 a.m. The Germans had broken our line and we had to be in reserve to the lines that they (the Germans) were attacking. It was in the afternoon that orders came for our lads to reinforce the lines that were in most danger. So we all knew there was a move on, and we marched out, ready for the fray, little dreaming what was in store for us. We got there in good time to take up our position, and as darkness was setting in, the enemy let loose their heavy artillery, ours replying. Then the Huns fired that hellish liquid fire, and hell was let loose. The next 48 hours were indescribable, especially the first four hours. Gradually the noise heightened, and the air was rent by the scream and crash of shell, hundreds of big guns on both sides throwing death to us and to the enemy. We got the order to advance nearer to the enemy, and it was proper hell on earth. Shells were raining on us from all quarters. An officer, who is an expert on heavy artillery, says we were under the heaviest shell-fire that there has ever been out here. The officer says shells were falling at the rate of 5,000 an hour.

We kept the Huns at bay, and so did the regiments on our right and left. We were all pleased when daylight broke, but then it was an awful sight to see the dead and wounded. We lost a lot of officers and men, but I am sorry to say we do not know what the Huns lost. Their roll would be very heavy, for our artillery were right on the target, and I could see through a periscope from the trench we were in that our big guns were breaking their trenches to pieces. Every "iron ration" - that is the name we give the big shells our boys send over to the Germans - was telling them a friendly story, and they need one. In spite of their

Battlefield Burial
©Imperial War Museums (Q 820)

gas and their liquid fire our boys can hold them. The wind has been in our favour for some time, and I think we should be allowed to fight them with their own weapons.

Private Joseph Reardon, 10th Battalion Durham Light Infantry
Newcastle Evening Chronicle 27 August 1915

I dare say that by this time you will have heard of the great honour that has been conferred on the handful of men who remain out of the 6th. The great Kitchener has been to see us, inspect us, and talk to us. Wednesday will go down to posterity as the red-letter day of the battalion. During the morning of the fateful day, the adjutant and sergeant-major came and carefully overhauled each man, and threatened him with five years' field punishment if he moved more than an eyelash at the time when on the great parade, which was held in a field near the billet. Well, at last we were all lined up, and word came that K was approaching. Our brigadier-general and the adjutant (the colonel being on leave) went to the gate of the field and received him. My word, you should have seen the crowd he came with - M. Millerand, the French Minister of War, French Field-marshals, Belgian, Russian, and Italian staff generals, and others too numerous to mention. Kitchener then came round and inspected us, and I had a good look at him. He is not a scrap like the photos you see. He has a large, round, red face, is very tall and carries his head high. The French War Minister was in civilian clothes, and raised his hat to each soldier who had a South African ribbon on his breast. Kitchener's speech was a fairly good one. He apologised for having allowed us to go into action immediately on landing in France, and said he fully appreciated the value of the work we had done. He added that everyone at home was proud of us, and hoped that we would get reinforcements to make us up to full strength.

Private Robert Thompson, 6th Battalion Northumberland Fusiliers
Newcastle Evening Chronicle 28 August 1915

THE BATTLE OF LOOS

The Battle of Loos (25 September - 14 October 1915) was the largest allied offensive in 1915, and noted for the first use of poison gas by the British. Although there were initial gains, the lack of sufficient reinforcements and ammunition meant that overall little was achieved at a high cost in life.

I am pretty fair after the ordeal I have gone through. We got orders on the Saturday to reinforce. We put on our packs and got on to the road. We had been marching all the week towards the firing line. We got to a town two miles off the British trenches, and, of course, the British had broken the German lines then, and had them on the move. We saw the wounded Gordon Highlanders coming back. The British used the gas before attacking, and the attack commenced at 6.30 in the morning. We marched through a village before we got to Loos, and we met two big batches of German prisoners. Then we went a little further on, and extended on a line before Loos about 5 o'clock in the afternoon, when we got orders to move on, and got to the first British trenches. We crossed these, and to the first firing line, then over those trenches and over some barbed wire and big shell-holes on to the German front firing trench. But we were blocked, as the German trenches had been blown to pieces and were all ravelled with wire. They were full of Germans' bodies, so we were ordered to close on the road where the right of our line was. We then marched towards Loos, and went to the right and entered a German communication trench. Just before we got to the trench we found a German shell about two feet long which had not exploded. We went along the trench, and a short distance along there was lying a dead German. I did not know he was there until I was standing upon him. He was a big chap. We went along the trench until we came to what had been the German firing trench, but we could get no farther, as the trench was blocked up with Germans' bodies. While we were there the Germans commenced to shell the road on our left that we had marched along. That was the first taste of fire that I had had, and I can tell you their shells were whistling the "Keel Row" as they were passing over heads, but none burst near us. We then got orders to advance through Loos, and when we got there we got let in for a jolly peppering from their shrapnel shells and their snipers. We dodged from one side of the street to the other, the shells bursting about our ears, and the snipers were busy all the time. We were led up to the "pit" - you will have seen it mentioned in the papers. The German's had the range, and we got to know it too. We were led to a bank running along the line leading to Hill 70. We then got orders to lie flat, as the snipers were all over the show, and were throwing up green rockets which lighted up the place, and shooting at us while the flare was on us.

Lance-Corporal Robert Ward, Northumberland Fusiliers
Newcastle Evening Chronicle 7 October 1915

You may have seen by the papers that we were in the big advance that started on Saturday, Sept. 25. After five nights' marching, we got close to the firing line early on that morning, and we were in reserve. After a heavy bombardment, our first line advanced, and took the German trenches. We followed them up, and drove the Germans into a pit village. Then the real fight started, out of one house into another; and we bayoneted every Hun we saw. This lasted about two hours, and then we had the village cleared, except for the snipers, who must have been well hidden, as they started sniping our wounded as they were going back to be dressed. Some of us went back to hunt them out, and, mind, we showed them no mercy when we found them. They went on their knees, saying "Mercy! Me married," or "Me English." We "married" them all right, but it was with the bayonet.

Four of us climber up some pit pulleys called "Tower Bridge," and there were four snipers on the top. They never knew we were there till we got hold of them. We never used the bayonet on them; we lifted them up and dropped

them down the pit shaft; and they deserved all they got for shooting our wounded. By this time our men were out of the village, and half way up a hill, where we had a hard fight. We got over the hill in the afternoon, but when it got dark we had to retire and dig a trench which we held all day

Wrecked British Transport amongst the debris in a ruined street, Loos 30 September 1915
©Imperial War Museums (Q 28987)

Sunday and Sunday night; and then we were relieved on Monday morning all dead beat, but content; for we knew it was a great victory for us.

The Germans must have lost thousands killed and wounded; and there were a lot surrendered. The village was an awful sight; the streets were full of dead, and in some of the houses they hadn't room to fall down when they got killed. The only time I was a bit afraid was on Saturday night, when the Germans were shelling us with shrapnel. The noise they make would make anybody afraid when one is not used to it. We lost a lot of men, but they are nearly all wounded, so that is not so bad. We are having a rest now till we get equipped again, as we had to throw our packs off in the scrap. We will never have a fight like it again, as they say it is the biggest there has been in this war.

Stanley Relph
Newcastle Evening Chronicle 9 October 1915

You ask me for an account of the deed which gained my distinction. I will try to write you a brief account. On September 25 we attacked the German positions in front of Loos. I was picked out to follow the charging infantry, and unreel a telephone wire as I ran forward. This was for the purpose of keeping the artillery in touch with the infantry. This was successfully carried out, although the wire was broken several times by bursting shells. Each time it was broken, I had to return and mend it under a heavy fire. I passed through an anxious and very exciting two days, and returned to my battery without a scratch, for which I thank God. We are having bad weather just now, and our men are undergoing very great hardships. They are bearing it very cheerfully, and all are determined to do their best to win. It is wonderful how discipline and a strong sense of duty have changed our men from every sphere of life to the finest soldiers in the world.

Bombardier J. R Handyside, DCM, MM, D Battery, 71st Brigade Royal Field Artillery
Newcastle Evening Chronicle 11 December 1915

When the Germans counter-attacked, we mowed them down with our machine guns, and there were heaps of dead Germans all over the place. We had ten minutes' peace on the 27th ult. Two of our lads were lying between our lines and the German lines. They had been wounded in the legs three days earlier, and were shouting for help. This was about one o'clock in the afternoon. The Germans ceased firing while two of our lads went out to bring the wounded in. One of them walked over and saluted the German officer, and his men came over the parapet, returned the salute, and gave our lads three cheers.

Private W. Morgan, Durham Light Infantry
Newcastle Evening Chronicle 11 November 1915

GALLIPOLI

The Gallipoli Campaign, planned to open up a second front firstly by a naval attack and then by a military landing in Turkey, Germany's 'soft underbelly' in the east, although in theory a good idea, proved to be a major disaster. There were initial landings in April, followed by others in August and September, but the allied forces, including a strong contingent of Australian and New Zealand troops, failed to make significant progress. With the arrival of severe winter conditions, the decision was taken in December 1915 to evacuate the troops, a process completed in January 1916. In total 188,000 allied troops were killed, wounded or taken prisoner.

We left England on February 27, and the ship, when she steamed down the Bristol Channel, had 2,500 troops abroad. We reached Malta on March 9. From there we got to Lemnos, and after staying there a week we went on to Port Said. Eventually we went to the Suez defences, 60 miles from Port Said. We were there only four days, when the Turks came up in small numbers. We never got a chance to have a scrap then. We left again just after Easter Sunday. While we were up Sir Ian Hamilton inspected the troops and defences. I will not forget

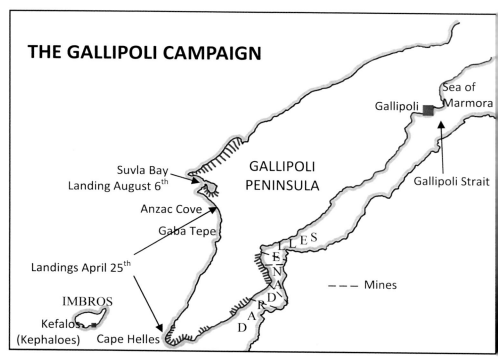

THE GALLIPOLI CAMPAIGN

Gallipoli

Sea of Marmora

Suvla Bay
Landing August 6th

GALLIPOLI
PENINSULA

Gallipoli Strait

Anzac Cove

Gaba Tepe

D E L L E S

Landings April 25th

— — — Mines

IMBROS

Kefalos
(Kephaloes)   Cape Helles

it, for we skirmished over the desert in a killing sun. It was there that we picked the Anson Battalion to make a landing party for the glorious 29th Division. We returned to Port Said, and after a few days the Ansons were separated from the rest of the R.N.D. and sent to Alexandria by rail. We camped there, and had a good time. We were split up again into companies. Some went on destroyers, some on battleships, and some on transports. We were on board the Mercian, and were supposed to take the 29th ashore in the boats which made the name that the Anson Battalion now holds. We shoved off back to Lemnos, and on March 18 left with other five transports to make a landing. The same day the *Irresistible*, the *Ocean* and the *Bouvet* were sunk, and that put the "tin hat" on the operations for that day. We returned to Lemnos, which is an island about 60 miles from Gallipoli, four hours' steam. We remained there until April 24. On the night of the 24th we again got off with a long line of transports. We could only guess where we were going. We steamed slowly, but the next morning we were wakened by the order to stand by with gear ready. We knew all about it by then, for we had heard the guns of the fleet. We went slowly and got to within half a mile of the scene of action. There we saw all. We were standing by to go ashore to what looked like certain death. The anchor was dropped, and then the *Triumph* put two or three sharp ones across our stern. The bullets from the shore were whizzing all over the ship, but no one was hit. We stood waiting orders to get to the boats, and some of the troops were landing on the various beaches allocated to them. We had to wait a long time before we got the order to fall in, and no sooner did we reach the gangway than we were recalled. I thank my lucky stars that I never attempted to land on the fateful day, April 25. We watched operations day and night, and I don't know how many Turks were left to tell the tale. The fleet didn't half give it them. On the following day I had a trip ashore with an officer, but the water's edge was enough for me. On the 28th we went ashore, as all the rest of our battalion had landed the first morning. We worked on the beach that day until we picked up the rest of the battalion. Then we were sent into the firing line, to back up the French.
It was on the 30th that we got a bit of our own back. The Turks came on in thousands, and the fleet got the tip to let go. The shells lit the place up nicely, and we could see them coming on. Then a shell would fall amongst them and leave a big hole. We thought we should never stop them coming. An order was given that if we retired we were to hold a little house. If the Turks had had the nerve to come on we should have been done for, because we had only a cliff to jump or to give in. Thanks to the splendid firing of the British Navy, we never had to retire. Things remained quiet until May 6 when, according to orders, we advanced 2,000 yards, but lost heavily. On June 4 we were again ordered to

advance. I lost my thumb-end in the charge. It took me about an hour to get back to the trench. I was helping a fellow up when I got a bullet through my cap, and the poor chap was killed at the same time. I was sent to Malta, and remained there until the end of July, when I got back to the Peninsula on August 15. From that date until I left I was in the machine-gun section. The Anson took part in the landing at Sulva (sic) Bay, but that was a picnic to the first landing. The Naval Division has done as much as any division out here.

Private A. G. Macgregor, Anson Battalion, Royal Naval Division
Newcastle Evening Chronicle 30 December 1915

Probably you would like to know something of the landing and fighting on the Gallipoli Peninsula. The Navy men have to do their bit on land. In the early morning of April 25, the order was sent round that all the landings would commence. The 29th Division - the Australians and the R.N.D. - men left the battleships for the tugs and mine-sweepers. As soon as the troops were off, all the Fleet went in a terrible shower of shells that swept the sea-shore and fortifications at Cape Helles, doing a great deal of execution amongst the Turks. Under cover of this hail of lead, the gallant lads left the tugs for the small boats, and commenced to row towards the shore. The Turks, who were cunningly concealed and protected by barbed wire, allowed our boys to come almost to the shore, then opened a rapid fire on them from Maxims and rifles. Hundreds of the lads fell into the water or were killed in the boats, but the remainder still carried on the work.

Never firing a shot, but sitting up stern and grim, they grounded the boats, and over they went into the water up to their chins. Some wading, some swimming, they reached the sandy strip of shore, and having fixed bayonets they started to climb the cliffs, all the time being mowed down. But British blood was being spilled in a just and glorious cause, so up the lads went, never flinching. The Turks gave ground, and some fled panic-stricken from these determined faces. The crest reached, our boys took breath and stock of the land in front. The daring feat of running the *River Clyde* aground was a masterpiece of naval and military ingenuity. Still it was not very successful, as the Turks were so strong and cleverly concealed, that it was instantaneous death to look out from the boat sides. Twice a landing was attempted from this boat, but every man was lost, so the attempt was left until darkness should help to cover their movements. In the night this landing was effected. The troops, except in one place, successfully consolidated their position, and defeated all the attacks the Turks flung against us at night. During the next two days we cleared all in front of us, for about two miles, and dug ourselves in. At this time I was attached to

V Beach Cape Helles from the River Clyde
©Imperial War Museums (Q 109150)

the *Royal George*. There is no doubt that the honours of the landing go to the 29th Division, supported by a few other troops and the R.N.D. All Britain should honour these lads, for truer Britons never wore shoe-leather.

On the 18th a general advance was ordered, and away they went, driving the Turks and their German commanders back for miles. The French also were doing well on the extreme right, and news came through that the Australians had successfully accomplished their landing at Gaba-Tepe, and had captured three guns and a number of prisoners. This news greatly cheered the advancing troops, and they swept all before them. But in spite of the gallant advance, the big guns of Achi-Baba kept booming and mowing the men down. And so heroically did the Turks defend their positions, that we had to pause. Ammunition and reserves were running low, and all we could do was to hold our positions.

Able Seaman J. H. Stelling, Howe Battalion, Royal Naval Division
Newcastle Evening Chronicle 2 September 1915

Our lads have done splendidly, and the Australians have made a name for themselves. Probably you have heard about our fight with the Turks. My company landed from a torpedo destroyer, and when we were in small boats the Turks spotted us and at once gave us a hot time from the top of the cliffs. The sailors at the oars pulled for their lives, but some were shot in the boats. We got enough to crawl up the bank, and forced the enemy back about a mile. They left three Krupp guns behind them.

One of my mates shot an officer dead, but we were knocked up and stiff after our cold dip. Soon the main body of Turks could be seen forming up their guns, and they gave us an awful time of it. Our brave chaps were simply slaughtered, and it was horrible to hear the wounded crying out for help which was not at hand. Their snipers were picking off our officers. My own officer was shot in the arm.

Private G.A. Bartlett, 9th Battalion 1st Australian Imperial Forces
Newcastle Evening Chronicle 3 June 1915

Fighting in a narrow place like this is, as you can guess, a great deal more spectacular than in France, as everyone who has been there says, and really there are some wonderful sights to see. We have seen a village burning during the night, another reduced to ruins in daylight, tons of bricks and earth hurled into the air by a lyddite shell - all sorts of awful sights. One often looks at scenes that are so strange that one wonders if one is awake or dreaming.

We live in a dug-out, a most magnificent residence, the result of blistered hands, aching backs, and sweating brows. There are two shelves in it, on which you put anything from your boots to the "unconsumed portion of the day's rations" (Field Service Pocket Book). The floor is handsomely graced with two box lids, and a cracked looking glass and a candle that persists in reclining at an angle of 45 degrees lend an air of homely, if not lavish, comfort. The poor candle cannot survive the heat of the day, and gradually takes an absurd list to one side, in fact, it sometimes bends nearly double. An ammunition box performs the duties of larder and seat, and if you discover you have not got the jam out, you merely rise (not too far or you will come into contact with the roof and crack your head prematurely), remove the lid, and extract the "preserves." Fortunately there is no lack of "tummy," as my partner calls it, and I am always ready to do full justice in that direction. We have the roof covered over with a tarpaulin and sandbags, but in spite of heated protests on our part, the roof has been made use of as a public thoroughfare, with the result that there is a decided danger of the bags collapsing between the beams. Never mind, we will soon remedy that. The flies are something awful, and every mealtime we have to make a general attack on them. After the enemy has been repulsed with heavy losses we drop the "door" - a waggon cover - and dine in peace. You see we are all in the best of health and spirits I am very grateful to say, and going on famously.

Sergeant L. Blake, Royal Marines, Royal Naval Division, dated 4 June 1915
Newcastle Evening Chronicle 3 July 1915

Dear Father - We have just got back to the rest camp after being five days in the firing line. Everything in the firing line is different from what I expected it to be. In the first place I always thought the trenches would be at least 80 yards apart, and that half of that distance would be covered with wire entanglement, but the trench that we were in was originally a Turkish fire trench, and when they retired they just moved into the communication trench, therefore their trench actually ran into ours. The end was blocked up with sandbags, but they still creep up and throw in hand grenades. Of course our boys can deal with them the same way. Well to give you an idea of life in the trenches, I will give you an ordinary day in the first line. Whenever it gets dark every man stands to and fixes his bayonet, and after a while if nothing brisk is going on every second man can rest (nobody is allowed to rest), but, of course, they take turn about, one hour on and one off. If anything is noticed they send up a star shell. It lights up the whole place, but it shows your position to the enemy just the same as you see theirs, so everybody has to keep out of sight, Of course some of the sentries can have a shot if there is anything to be seen. Well, just after dawn everybody has to be on the lookout, and after it is daylight bayonets are unfixed and one man in six is on sentry. The rest can sleep, but there is food, water and ammunition to be brought in, and as you have all your cooking to do, you don't get much rest. Of course, that is on a quiet day. You might have to be firing both day and night. The second night we were in, our tanks advanced a little, and thinking we were going to do the same, the Turks kept up a rapid fire all night. We went into the trenches as if it was an everyday occurrence. Nobody was excited when we fired on for the first time. You would have thought that everybody wanted to fire, but still I never saw anybody fire unless he had something to fire at. The enemy's snipers were a bit troublesome at times, but a good many snipers were sent to the happy hunting grounds.

Lance-Corporal J. Frater, 4th K.O.S.B.
Berwick Advertiser, 13 August 1915

I have been in Turkey just over a month and have had all kinds of experiences. The greatest of all, however, was on the 4th [June] when we made our first bayonet charge. We were told the night previously that we were to charge at

10 a.m. The artillery and ships began a light bombardment, which lasted until 11.20. We all rose then, waved our bayonets, and cheered and shouted for all we were worth. We got into our trenches again, and at 11.30 the artillery began in earnest, and I wouldn't have changed places with those Turks for thousands. At noon we were scrambling over our parapets, not knowing what was going to happen to us. I hadn't gone far when I saw one of my comrades lying dead. By this time the bullets and shrapnel were flying like hail. When I look back on it all it makes me thank God more and more that I am still alive. When the Turks saw us coming many vanished by way of their communication trenches, others ran for it, and as soon as we got near them they were soon settled with. A few remained in the trench and were either shot or taken prisoners. This, of course was their first line of trenches. I passed this and was just nearing their second line when I got shot through the thigh. The wound is about ¼ inch in diameter. I think this must be owing to their using explosive bullets. I managed to get safely back to the base, but it took me about an hour per mile, and that with assistance. Now I am comfortable here, and well looked after, and my wound is getting on all right now.

Private J. Henderson, 6th Battalion, Manchester Regiment, from a hospital in Malta
Newcastle Evening Chronicle 22 July 1915

This is the longest rest that we had out of the trenches; we have already had a fortnight. The worst thing here is the fly trouble - there are millions of flies. You would have laughed if you had seen the pancakes I made. I had some flour given me and also some currants and raisins. I make the flour up into a paste, and then put in the currants and raisins. Joe brought six eggs and a tin of milk from the canteen. Eggs are 1s. 6d. a dozen, and the milk 1s. a tin. I put an egg and about a tin of milk in, and then put the lot into a pan on the fire amongst some bacon grease. The first pancake was all right. The second one was too thick. I had no grease left, but I thought it would not matter. Well, the outside was like cinders, and the inside was soft, just paste. I let some of my mates taste it; you should have seen their faces. I am going to try to make a pudding - a currant pudding - next time. I will send you some to taste. We get milk in our tea now.

Seaman William Best, Hawke Battalion, Royal Naval Division
Newcastle Evening Chronicle 25 August 1915

I landed on the Gallipoli Peninsula on the Sunday morning at 3 o'clock, and went to my tent with my bag and baggage. Who should I see when I came out but my brother Len sitting on a boat, writing to me. He was delighted to see me. He had been on duty in the trenches a good bit and his company had been sent to the rest camp. All his clothes had been blow (sic) off with a shell, and he had nothing but what he stood up in. so I gave him a shirt, a towel, and a pair of socks, and set him up again. When he went to get a bath he had to dry himself on his shirt, and then wait till the sun dried his shirt. I went back with him to the camp and saw Jimmie Fleming, Isaac Rothery, and Jack Naisbet, all Browney men. We had our tea together in a dug-out, and the shells were flying all the time. We are in good health, but nearly like niggers with the sun. Yesterday there was a big battle. I was looking after the wounded and taking them from the shore to different ships. I was at it for nearly twenty-four hours, and it was the most exciting time of my life, as the shells were bursting all round the boat. You could hear them coming, and had to get cover and wonder where they were going to drop. Talk about moving pictures, they are not in it.

Stoker Will Brown, Royal Navy
Newcastle Evening Chronicle 26 July 1915

I have seen in the newspapers long accounts of the landing at Suvla Bay on the night of August 6. As you already know, or have guessed, that was my baptism of fire. We embarked at the island with the two first battalions of our division (just the bearers of the field ambulance). We were on little lighters. They are very small and have gangway at the bows just like our ferry. We were packed

Evacuation of the wounded from ANZAC Cove in Gallipoli by boat.
Ref: 1/4-008784-F. Alexander Turnbull Library, Wellington, New Zealand.

like herrings down below and on deck, and no speaking or smoking was allowed. For nearly three hours we sailed like this. The sun set about 7 o'clock, and it was pitch dark from 7.15 p.m. until midnight, when a glorious moon rose. It was while it was dark that the deed was done. I was one of those down below, and I felt fine and slept for nearly two hours. Then we began to feel a little excited. Suddenly we heard a yell from the wheel, "Lookout forward! Stand tight!" and the boat ran full-tilt aground, making a terrible row on the gravel the chains seemed to make an awful rattle as they dropped the gangway. Just then I heard my first bullet fired. It banged against some sheet iron on deck and caused a sudden move amongst all on board. We all jumped off the lighter with our stretchers and lay down on the sand about 100 yards to the right of the boat. A dozen or two rifles cracked at intervals, but our chaps never fired back. They were about 30 yards farther along the sands than we were, and were all lying flat with bayonets fixed. There was a level stretch of about 100 yards of sand in front of us and then a small hill. A few snipers were scattered on the level, potting at us, while the others were digging like the deuce on top of the hill. Later, their half-made trench made a decent cover for some of our wounded. For what seemed hours we lay like this. Two more lighters came ashore behind us and more further up the shore, but we could only hear them, for it was too dark to see. Orders were given to the infantry, and they got up and advanced slowly. The snipers appeared to retreat towards the hill, and on the way they managed to drop one or two of our troops. Then we started the charge, our men yelling and shouting as loud as they could. They took the hill at the double, B Section went over the ground right away and brought in nine men, one Turkish officer and three men, and left seven dead. L----- and I got lost a bit with our stretcher... We put down the stretcher and lay down beside it. Within a few minutes a column of our infantry came past us, about a dozen yards off. You know how they march with outposts on the flanks. Well we had two of them doubling at us with bayonets at the ready and shouting "Here you are, Sir." I got a bit of a shock at first, but I shouted, "It's all right." By then a lieutenant had come up, and he seemed a bit surprised when I told him we were a R.A.M.C. patrol. He replied, "You fellows ashore already," and then went off, while I told the corporal of the outpost that he would find some more of our chaps farther on, and that he had better be careful with his bayonet. Just then the moon started to show itself, and then we began to get some of our first shrapnel. We watched the flashes, and never thought of getting hit. We joined with some more of the section and went over the first hill and found another small rise. On top of this our troops were engaged in heavy rifle fire. They had to hold this position until all the division was landed. We got tons of shrapnel during the next few hours, and plenty wounded men. The Turks were not in very great numbers, but they had strong positions. We soon got them on the run on the Saturday morning and some murder was done crossing the Salt Lake.

Private R. Steedman, Royal Army Medical Corps.
Newcastle Evening Chronicle 19 October, 1915

When it rains here, it doesn't forget to rain, three drops and you are wet through; but we don't get much of it. It still keeps uncomfortably hot. We are getting fed pretty decently just now. You will be surprised when I tell you I ventured may (sic) hand in domestic affairs. I made a roly-poly jam pudding the other day, and, not being in possession of a white cloth, I was obliged to boil it in a khaki cloth, and when the pudding came out it was khaki. It went down all right. I will be teaching you the French language on my return home, provided I am spared, as I am great friends with the French. I often indulge in a meal of rice and coffee with them; it is a welcome change from tea. Will you put a tin of salmon in one of the parcels, as fish is quite a luxury out here. We can purchase eggs at 1s. 3d. a dozen.

A.H. Arthur Tutin, Machine Gun Section, Hawks Division, Royal Naval Division
Newcastle Evening Chronicle 3 September 1915

I expect you will have got to know before you receive this that I have been knocked over. It happened after the worst was over, about two o'clock in the afternoon. We were attacking a place, and had to cross open ground without one bit of cover. It was just like a thunderstorm, only it was raining lead instead of water. It was terrible, and the lads were falling all over the place. We got as far forward as possible and then started firing. The worst part about it was that when we got there amongst the long grass and bushes the Turks set them on fire. We retired about fifty yards through the fire, and stuck there. The 8th Northumberland Fusiliers did their bit that day.
Two hours later we captured a woman sniper, and she was dyed green. She was simply laden with ammunition. The bullet I was struck by was from her; it went through my thigh, and came out just below my left hip. It was very painful, but I feel a lot better now. They are very kind to us on the hospital-ship, and nothing is a trouble to them.

Corporal J. Tait, 8th Battalion Northumberland Fusiliers (wounded 10 August 1915)
Newcastle Evening Chronicle 9 September 1915

I had about 30 men under me when one of them stepped upon a land mine. He was only the second man from me. Poor fellow, he was wounded in five different places, but he still lives, so far as I know. When they exploded that mine, it knocked the man next to me clean out of time for a quarter of an hour. There was not a mark upon him. I was lifted fully 10 feet into the air and landed again on my feet. I was very lucky to get clear of them, as we afterwards found four more unexploded mines in the same place. Now these mines were laid in front of some Turkish trenches, and, needless to say, they belong to us now. Well, after a blow for a few minutes to get ourselves pulled together again, we went after them again, and, by God, it was a bit of all right. They fairly swept the ground with shrapnel, but, undaunted, our fellows kept on, and fairly carried the position at the bayonet point. We slept, or rather, I should say, tried to sleep, on the battle field, for fighting was taking place first here and then there, so we could not tell when we would be getting a move on. Well, at last day came upon us, and, by the way, it happened to be Sunday morning. Having started work on Friday night, you can form some idea of what we were like for something to eat. Although we had tea, sugar, bully beef, and biscuits with us, as well as Oxo tablets, which are one of the finest things issued as soldiers' rations, we had not tasted food since starting operations, for water was scarce, and we were afraid to eat. But, as other troops had landed since we started, they brought food up to us. We got the order to retire to the beach, where we rested all day on Sunday. Nobody ever enjoyed a drink of tea as did the lads who had been tried and proved true to the call. I learnt afterwards that the general officer was very pleased with our conduct under fire.

Sergeant D. Burns
Newcastle Evening Chronicle 13 September 1915

I am trying to get my own back by popping over a Turkish sniper, but he is too clever for me. He makes us keep our heads below the parapet., seeing he nails everyone who shows up his "napper." He always kills. Explosive bullets. His latest victim was a Major. When he fires a shot half a dozen bullets patter round the loophole he is firing from. Whenever he puts up his periscope to see how the land lies, he gets a bullet through it or past it from the first man who sees it. If the shot misses, he signals a miss, and he seems to like a joke. He puts his head-gear on a stick, and holds it up for us to have a shot at.

One of the 4th King's Own Scottish Borderers
Southern Reporter 23 September 1915

People in England think there is no winter in Turkey, but that is a fairy tale. We have had two thunderstorms here lately, and I shall remember them as long as I live. The first one wrecked every dug-out in the battery, except mine, and it failed there, because I am dug into a rock. The rain came down in torrents, and in ten minutes there was about six feet of water running down the gulley as it is called... At present the bottom is a river of mud. At night, after the storm, bread, meat, forage, dead bodies and all sorts of things come floating down towards the sea. Two days later they asked for a volunteer to take a message to a place near the trenches, and as it was fine at the time I volunteered. I had not got half-way there when another storm came on, and in two minutes I was drenched to the skin. It rained so hard that I had to get off my horse and walk. I was up to the ankles in mud, and bullets were whizzing past me in all directions. Eventually I delivered the despatch safely and got back to my dug-out like a drowned rat at 2 o'clock only to find the same thing as two days previously.

Driver M. W. White, Royal Field Artillery
Newcastle Evening Chronicle 20 December 1915

When we landed the heat was unbearable, and even at night the sand was warm. We pitched our camp on a beach, and have never stirred from there. We proceeded straight away to get our hospital going, erecting one hospital tent after another, until the place assumed quite terrific proportions in our eyes. We have kept up quite a big field hospital ever since. We are quite near to the firing lines, and the shells in their progress often whistle overhead. So far, however, the Turks have shown us great consideration, and it has only been very occasionally that their shells have fallen amongst us. The weather is quite Christmassy now - cold and windy, though, so far, accompanied by very little rain. What little we have had, however, was quite enough. It never rains here but it pours. A tent won't keep you dry, for the rain beats through the canvas in no time. The worst think we have to encounter, however, is the sandstorm, and it is no joke. In the regimental office where I do my work we had, last time, "to shut up shop altogether."

We closed the tent and sat tight until meal times, when we put on gas helmets to protect us from the sand, ran over to the cook house, and then ran back with our meals, got into the tent and stayed there until the storm abated. It was impossible to open a book, for before you could put pencil to it, it lay an inch deep in sandy grit. Still the patients had to be dressed, fed, and generally looked after; and there was not one of us, from the Major downwards, who did not feel thankful when, towards night, the wind went down and everything was calm, except the sea, which kept lashing the beach in fury until morning. Still, with all its drawbacks, it is a wonderful experience to be for once away entirely from civilised and civilian people, for we are encamped on the edge of a desert valley. The nearest native village can just be seen in a cleft in the hills with the aid of powerful glasses and that was long ago deserted and a mass of ruins.

Letter to Mr. T. G. Carr of Newcastle
Newcastle Evening Chronicle 22 December 1915

MEDICAL CARE

Care for the wounded was the responsibility of the Royal Army Medical Corps who provided doctors, orderlies, stretcher bearers and field ambulances. Firstly the wounded went through a field dressing station, before being moved to a casualty clearing station. There soldiers were treated and either sent back to their units or in more serious cases transferred, often by train, to base hospitals either in France or back in the UK, in the case of Western Front injuries; most wounded from Gallipoli were transferred by ship to Alexandria. Nursing was provided both by trained nurses working under the auspices of the Red Cross, and volunteers - Voluntary Aid Nurses or VADs.

The patients are very cheerful and nearly all longing to get better and return to the front again, all so keen to be at work. You never hear them complain or murmur about their wounds, and some have very bad ones. It is marvellous, I think, how bright and cheerful they keep. I have had many things from the Red Cross up to date, such nice, useful garments, pyjamas, bed jackets, socks, slippers, small white blankets, dressing gowns, etc., as well as such luxuries as toilet soap, cigarettes, and other things mentioned on the list I sent you. All come in useful and are such an addition to the patients' comforts.

We have got a good many German prisoners - some badly wounded, others slightly. All are bright and cheerful and very pleased to be with the English. Some talk a little English; others can't speak any. We have no French patients; they go to their own hospitals. Some days we take in as many as 100 or over, and, of course, send home a great many. The wounds are mostly bullet or shrapnel; the latter leaves a very nasty wound. The men treasure the bullets when they are extracted, and are so proud of them, and no wonder, they have fought so well. Their experience in the fighting line is very much what you read of in the papers - days of heavy fighting, often at great odds.

The Matron of a BEF Hospital
Newcastle Journal 1 October 1914, originally in the Morning Post

But we shall all appreciate dear old England a thousand times more when we return to our good "comfy" homes. I must say I am awfully glad I came out here. Oh! there is so much to do, and the Tommies are so grateful. Poor boys, they seem to love to have us, and one feels one cannot do enough for them. They are so fine and brave and never complain at all about anything: always smiling and seeing the bright side of life - even when wounded. One feels proud to be a Briton, and the French people just adore them.

We just live on the trains. It takes days from the boat to the front: we load the patients on and then bring them here and go back empty. It is VERY hard work, as the majority are stretcher cases, but then we sleep going back after we get things straightened. We go right up, and I shall never forget the first time I heard the guns open: it was most awful: one simply couldn't realize it. It was about

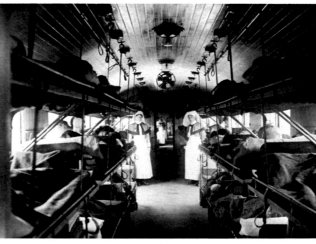

Hospital Train
©Imperial War Museums (Q 33447)

midnight, just when we arrived. Now, strange thought it seems, we feel funny down here away from the noise of it, but love the peacefulness. Oh, the stories one hears from the poor Tommies, and the officers too, who are just as fine! One told me to-day before he left us that he was just going to live for the day when he came back here again, poor soul, he had lost his left arm, but he said he was proud of it, and thought it was the finest act a man could do - to die for his country.

It really does one good to meet so many many fine, brave, heroic men. One forgets the sadness in the midst of so much greatness, and our only thought is how much can we do to try and make them more "comfy" in the long train journey. My word! they do appreciate us, poor boys! It is always the same when we say "good-bye!" - "Oh, sister, do come to England with us!" I am sorry to confess one sometimes does wish just to go with them and have a peep at you all, but COME STRAIGHT BACK HERE AGAIN to do what one can until this awful war is ended.

We are going up a good deal further this time. Last journey we were within three miles of the fighting line, but as they drive them back, the further we follow up. We are all frightfully proud at being chosen for train duty at the front. ----- is in charge, and there are doctors, nurses, orderlies, and the usual domestic staff. Of course we are on rations - tinned meat and biscuits - like the soldiers, with butter as a treat, but we feel we love to be treated like them. We have a great feed when we get down here once a week, not to forget a bath, which we have to pay a franc for....

I got some papers from you at one of the stations on the way down. The soldiers simply devour them, poor souls - not to mention us. Anybody you know knitting socks or making shirts, ask them to send them here. Really, they are more wanted on the trains than anywhere else. We get the men straight off the trenches, sometimes with hardly any clothes, and socks and boots which have not been off for some time. If they just address them to me, I will get them all right. Really the hospitals are nearly all equipped well. If they only saw the poor men's faces when we get their boots off and their clean, warm things on, they would feel more than repaid, I am sure. Many people are making them, but don't know where they are most needed. In the hospitals they have warm beds, but in the trains it is very different. I must stop, or the boat will be off. The bell has gone, so I must get the boatman to run with this for me.

Eva Schofield, a nurse on a hospital train
Morpeth Herald, 16 October 1914

My day; up at 6.30, and of late working in my hut at a temperature of over a hundred degrees up to 8 p.m. has taken it out of me. Our men are "Isoles," which means lonely ones, men who go and come from the trenches, men who are rejoining their lost regiments, men coming from all over France. Some are very nerve worn and must rest, some only just convalescent, some feverish, some lame. They all come to us, and we generally keep them for periods varying from 36 hours to four or five days. Some go on in a few hours only. We have every kind through our hands - Moroccans, Turcos, Senegalese, Tirailleurs, and all the purely French men as well. I have had the most wonderful study of people under most extreme circumstances, and have learnt a lot. Humans are most wonderful creatures; they are all over the same - simply children - rather naughty at times, and have to be treated as such. It's a sad sight to see them go off silently into the night, knowing half will never return. We get great numbers arriving too; they come in done to the world sometimes, and can hardly stagger up to the hut for some coffee or chocolate, and then they fall in heaps and sleep where they can in the workshop, which serves as accommodation. Take them all round, they are a most grateful, decent lot, but when you have every type and colour and 700 to 800 a day coming and going, you can guess a few give a little trouble. Oh, I have heard and seen some terrible things from them - photos taken on the spot that are too awful, things they tell you sometimes when you can talk quietly to them that are blood-curdling. One has got steady nerves, thank God; one needs them, I can tell you. I got a permit to go over a certain hospital...... and, oh, it is burnt in my mind all I saw there! .... Every type of horror this carnage can produce........ Some (to me the saddest of all) were men who had lost their nerves completely (for a while anyway) and who sobbed at the least kind word. One poor fellow held his hand to me and I took it and said, "It's all right, old fellow I understand." He squeezed my hand and then turned away and sobbed. I longed to fold them all up in my arms and comfort them and tell them it would pass, but how well I knew the agony of nerve all bare and quivering. And no one can help; one must fight the battle alone - each one is alone when the supreme test comes, alone and yet not alone if only one can hang on to the thought, but it's so hard. Some poor souls I saw at rest for ever, some coming from the operating room, some going there. I think I saw everything: they were short-handed and working grandly for the poor men. Some I saw gasping and fighting for every breath, black and blue from this gas poisoning. If it were not for the wonders that are being done for them, one could hardly have borne it, but one gets more steady

Letter to Mrs. Thirladean, Selkirk, from a lady working in France
Southern Reporter 1 July 1915

Lieut ----- and myself had to mark off some new trenches last Saturday and we went out at 9.30 in the morning. We should have returned at 12.30, but when we got finished he wanted to see as much of the German positions as he could, and although I told him it was risky going there, he would go, and, poor chap, he was killed. I got some nasty wounds, one inside the left leg below the knee, and one above right knee, and two in the left arm between elbow and wrist. I called for help, and Captain ----- of the Border Regiment crept out and dragged me about 20 yards into a hollow, full of dirty water. He got my wounds roughly dressed and left me, telling me to lie still, till dark, when a stretcher would come for me. It was about 11.45 a/m/ when I was hit, and I lay till nearly midnight - 12 hours - before the stretcher-bearers got me. I was carried over all sorts of ground, till we got to a dressing station. Eventually after motor and train rides I arrived here (Le Treport). I went through an operation, and had the bullets taken out, wounds cleaned and dressed, and I am (according to the doctor) very lucky to be on top. I will be sent over to England as soon as I am able to be moved, which may not be long if I go on all right. This is an awful experience - bed. I am on chicken and stout for dinner, and port wine twice a day, and eggs. It is splendid here - a nice little place right on the sea, with banks 300 feet high. The nurses are very kind. A Gateshead girl and a Prudhoe lady are here as Red Cross sisters.

Corporal Thomas Anderson, Northumbrian Division, Royal Engineers
Newcastle Evening Chronicle 8 July 1915

The wounded we did get were all badly maimed, and many had lost arms and legs. All the cases we got had been wounded with shrapnel with one exception, which was a bullet wound. We worked all night in the temporary hospital dressing the wounded as they came in, and the doctors were continually operating - amputating arms and legs. Again at four o'clock we were ordered to retire but owing to the serious condition of the wounded it was impossible to remove most of the cases. Where it was possible we sent the bearers away with wounded men, and the male nurses were left behind to look after those men who still required dressing. At six o'clock in the morning the Germans started bombarding the town. Houses round about us were soon knocked down, but fortunately the hospital escaped with slight damage to the roof. The Germans afterwards said that they had done their utmost to avoid firing on the hospital after they had seen our flag. I'm not so sure of that, because a substantial house in front of us was never struck, and I think it was either bad shooting or our luck that caused us to escape. Two of our R.A.M.C. men were wounded during the bombardment - one in the back and the other in the leg.

When the Germans came up to us we discovered they were in charge of two

Stretcher bearers bringing in a wounded man over muddy ground
©Imperial War Museums (CO 2202)

officers, one of them could speak English…. He said "We do not fight the Red Cross people. You are all right here while the Red Cross flag is flying." He asked all about the wounded, how many we had, and he then went into the hospital to inspect the wounded. We were ordered to carry outside all the arms and ammunition belonging to the wounded and the German soldiers proceeded to smash the rifles by damaging the bolts… One German took a rifle by the barrel and tried to break the butt against the kerbstone, but the rifle went off and the bullet went through his abdomen. He dropped. There was no more trying to break the rifles after that.

Sergeant Alexander Tarbet, R.A.M.C.
Berwick Advertiser, 9 July 1915

You were asking how my promotion affected me, and whether it placed me in greater danger or less. Well, it does not affect me a great deal but it means an increase of 7d. a day in my pay. When I was a sergeant, I was in charge of the stretcher squads of my own section. Now that I am staff-sergeant I am the senior non-commissioned officer of the section, and have to look after things in general, and arrange all the various duties, etc. A field ambulance is composed of three sections (A, B, and C), and each section is complete in every detail, and with its own transport; so that any one section can be away from the other two to act independently. This is what we have been doing lately, and when such is the case one of my duties is to see to getting the rations in. When we are working together as a unit, the quartermaster-sergeant is the man who looks after the rations. I have, however, been up with the stretcher-bearers a good deal lately, and at times it has been pretty hot. We had another move about a week ago and are now at a much quieter part of the line. Here we can go about right up to the trenches in the ambulance cars without anything serious happening. We get a few stray bullets now and again, but nothing to what we were having a week or two ago. Before coming to this part of the line we had to send large parties of stretcher-bearers out every night. Our ambulance cars could take us only so far along the road - owing to the shelling of the same - and we had to walk from the cars to the trenches, taking what cover we could by dodging along by the hedges, etc. We were often getting bullets over from three different directions, and it seems marvellous that we have had so few casualties. One night when I was out it was particularly warm. The Germans had their machine guns in action, and we had to stay in a trench for a few hours before things were quiet enough for us to proceed with our work. We do all our work at night, but it is quite light owing to the flash lights thrown up from the trenches. We have had only six of our own men wounded so far, and these, I am pleased to say, have all been more or less slight cases. We are also running two hospitals just now. At one we dress all the wounded that come in, and then send them off to the general hospitals. At the other we treat sick cases until they are well enough to rejoin their companies. At our last billet we had about 200 German prisoners quite near us. Two or three of them were fairly old men, but on the whole they looked quite good. They needed a good wash and a shave, but were just what you would expect our own men to look like after being in the trenches some time.

Staff Sergeant Peckard (Newcastle and Gateshead Gas Company)
Newcastle Evening Chronicle 15 July 1915

We are now full up. Including to-day's number we have nearly 1,000 on board. The sight would make the hardest heart bleed. The men are all so brave. It's impossible to describe the nature of the wounds. How I wish you could see the men in my ward - great big, fine fellows. Quite a number are Scots, one or two are Irish, and four Australians. Some are without arms, others with a leg or a foot missing. I think we nurses see the blackest side of the war. But I love the work and only hope I shall have the chance of staying on a hospital ship. We proceed to Alexandria to-morrow morning. We will leave the wounded there, and I expect to return back to the Dardanelles. It has been most exciting. The shells have been bursting round us each day, and during the night also we could hear them whistling as they flew past or dropped near us.

Nurse Lizzie Carruthers, Hospital ship 'Neuralia'
Newcastle Evening Chronicle 24 July 1915

I am as well as can be expected under the circumstances, as I was a passenger on the ill-fated hospital ship "Anglia." We were all very bright on board with thoughts of home. A chap I had made friends with on the boat had a broken shoulder. We had just had some sandwich and some tea. We went up on deck again, and got nicely settled down behind the second funnel when someone shouted out "There's the cliffs of Dover," and just then - bang! We had struck a mine. We knew pretty well the ship was doomed. The cry went out "Women first." There was no panic although we felt the ship was sinking fast. I climbed on the rail and saw a boat racing to our rescue. She came quite close and took 30 or 40 people off.

I then saw one of our boats launched, but it immediately turned upside down, and many went straight to the bottom, poor souls. I then off with my top-coat and tunic, loosened my boots and climbed on to the fender, that is the ledge that runs near the water-line below the port-holes. I tried to coax my pal to dive for it. But I suddenly remembered that he had only one arm, so I climbed back again, went below, got a lifebelt, and laid it down on the bed till I found another for my friend, but when I looked back it was gone. At last I found another, and put it on. I

Sinking of the "Anglia" off Folkestone 17 November 1915
©Imperial War Museums (Q 22867)

got back on deck and put the other life-belt on that poor chap and helped him over the top rail. Then I got on to the fender again, and saw two chaps smashed up by the propeller. I helped my chum as well as I could, and said to him "Are you ready to dive?" But he was afraid, so I bade him good-bye. He bade me good bye and good luck. Oh my that cold plunge! I shudder even now at the thought of it. When I came to the surface I found my left leg had taken the cramp, but a raft was within reach of my left hand. I grabbed it, and was drifting about, which was terrible in the icy water. Then, after what seemed an eternity, I was hauled on to a boat. I then helped to pull in the boat. We looked about and saw no one else in the water, so we pulled to the "Hazard". I was hauled on board and got my left leg bruised in the process.

I thought I was never going to stop shivering again, but hot whisky, brandy, rum, milk, etc., together with being wrapped in a blanket and somebody putting a cigarette into my mouth made me feel much better. Fancy, I lost everything but my life. But I am content to have my life. We were put off at Dover, wrapped in blankets, and put on to a hospital train. The next thing I remember was being in a comfortable bed in a hospital, waited on hand and foot.

I wonder what became of my poor chum. Every bone in my body is aching, and I am afraid you would hardly know me. There was a message from the King to the survivors, but I did not hear it, as the nurse said I was asleep, but she is going to read it to me. Now this is the finish of my experience. Here I must lie, and have hot milk and eggs, etc., packed into me.

Private A. E. Reynolds, 2nd Durham Light Infantry
Newcastle Evening Chronicle 25 November 1915

THE WAR IN THE AIR

Air warfare was in its infancy, but both airships and planes were used by both sides, for aerial reconnaissance, bombing and dog fights.

I forgot to mention that I have seen three aeroplanes brought down. The first, a German, was just after the battle of -----. It had been hit by shrapnel, the planes were holed, and the aviator and his companion were wounded. Pluckily they tried to volplane to their own lines, but it was very close when crossing our dug-outs, and naturally the boys finished it off with rifle fire. One of the men in the aeroplane died on his way to hospital; the other was still alive when last I heard of him, but was very seriously wounded.

The second was an English one, and he came down a mile from us, but was uninjured. The third was a German, and it occurred last night. It was looking around well up in the air, and soon the French were firing one of their anti-air craft guns at it. For a long time the shots were going wide, but at last a cry went up: "That's hit him." Sure enough, he was hit. Down he swooped like a stone from what appeared to be about 2,000 feet. Then the speed was gradually checked.

How the aviator regained control of the machine passes comprehension, but still he could not prevent the fall, and his machine was seen to have taken fire. It dropped some distance from us, but we learnt that it had landed on some trees; both men were killed, and the machine was burnt out. Enemies they may be, but let us give credit even to an enemy. The manner in which the airmen checked the fall was marvellous.

Corporal John Johnson, 4th Northumberland Fusiliers
Newcastle Journal 1 June 1915

June 3rd. - We are for the moment in the same great wood where we were before. It is entirely composed of oak trees - not large ones- and comparatively thin. You see if troops are in a wood they can't be spotted by aeroplanes, which are one of the great factors in this war. Aeroplanes, German ones of course, chiefly - keep flying over - marking position of trenches, and trying to find out position of guns, spotting troops in movement or in bivouac, noting any passage of transport along roads etc. Where they do spot anything, in no time their great guns let fly, then the air is full of shells, and hell begins. Yesterday I was with an artillery officer registering for howitzers. We were in the open for a minute or two, but with a hedge behind, so that we did not show out in silhouette. Then we jumped into the trench, and just in time, for three shells, one after the other, as hard as they could be fired, came just where we had been a few minutes before. They must have very good observers, and a splendid telephone service to every point. There is no doubt they are very thorough in their savagery also, as well as in proper war.

Anonymous Berwick Officer with 7th Northumberland Fusiliers
Berwick Advertiser, 11 June 1915

We have had some attacks on us by "Taubes," and one especially useful one on Whit-Monday. They were disguised as our ones in every particular, and so got safely past all the signal stations. The bombs were the first sign anything was wrong; you never heard such a noise. It was in the morning, and very hot and a brilliant sky. I was in my room having half an hour off when suddenly I heard the most awful noise and violent burst of booming. I ran to the window and saw nothing but my neighbours all looking up in the air and over the country. Then I heard a very faint sound of engines and suddenly saw a flash like lightning, followed by an explosion which shook my little house and jumped me off my feet with concussion, and a great column of smoke and flame. Then I knew and ran downstairs just as the people called out, "Come quickly, they are on us." I went over to my soldiers, and then the fun began, crash, bang, all over the place. Soon our men were up in the air and began to chase and shoot at them. Crack went the guns down below; crack, crack from the planes in the air. It was most keenly exciting. One time we had one just above our heads, and it was a very tense moment wondering when and where the bomb would fall. Luckily the Taube was very high up and one of our men also on the chase, so the aim was not so accurate, and it fell over the wall which surrounds us into the field, and none of us were hurt. There were fires caused, but no lives lost. It's a queer feeling never being quite sure what will come along any day for one.

Letter to Mrs. Thirladean, Selkirk, from a lady working in France
Southern Reporter 1 July 1915

I am sending my impressions of an aeroplane duel witnessed from the trenches in northern France. It was early evening of a day to which both rain and sunshine had each with varying success struggled for predomination. The result was indecisive, and heavy clouds darkened a good part of the sky. Not at all an ideal night for aeroplane reconnaissance, yet it must be done, for the artillery had laid quiet most of the day, and the enemy's reserves gradually massing well in the rear of their first lines must be dispersed. The aeroplane gradually mounted higher and higher in wide circles, unnoticed by the men in the trenches and so far by the enemy's anti-aircraft guns. Under cover of the clouds, which prove an effective screen, the pilot steered his machine well over the enemy's lines. Suddenly on the still air breaks out the rattle of a machine gun, which, by its sound, proceeds from the clouds, and causes the men in the trenches to gaze upward, forgetting for the moment the enemy in the opposing trenches a short distance away. These men know well what the rattle portends, and excitedly call their colleagues from their dug-outs, for after a quiet day an air duel, which they know to be in progress, should amply compensate for the lack of excitement during the day. Eyes eagerly scan the darkening sky, and two aeroplanes are dimly seen emerging from behind the clouds, circling round each other and each seeking for advantage in position, thence dealing a death blow to the enemy. Crack go the machine guns and suddenly one of the machines makes off, apparently damaged by that last fusillade. As it darts away three little balls of flame drop from it, and quickly disappear in smoke. Has the aeroplane been really damaged and are the balls of flame a prelude to a sheet of flame gradually enveloping the machine and its occupants and then that sickening fall to the earth so far beneath? No, for the aeroplane still continues its flight, and as the distance between it and the hostile craft increases, bang, bang go "Archibald's" as the anti-aircraft guns are called, and shells burst in dangerous proximity to the triumphant aeroplane.

The little balls of flame had been a signal for assistance to the waiting gunners and they for revenge try to wreck the now pursuing victor. But what is that other dark shape appearing on the scene? Another aeroplane, friend or foe, which? It promptly comes to the aid of the vanquished aeroplane, which seeks safety in flight, and itself engages the attention of the other late combatant, which comes bravely to the attack emboldened by its previous success. Back and forward, round and round circle the two machines, turning and twisting in a truly masterly manner. Again breaks on the air the sound of the spiteful machine guns, and the watchers below hold their breath, awaiting the crippling of one or the other of the machines. But they are disappointed for darkness is quickly descending, and as the sound of the firing grows more indistinct the aeroplanes gradually vanish from sight, seeking a final home in another part of the line, where the watchers there may witness something decisive.

Signaller Thomas Pratt, 5th Northumberland Fusiliers
Newcastle Evening Chronicle 29 October 1915

Dogfight over Dunsfold
Courtesy of Brooklands Cars Ltd

INDEX OF PEOPLE

The names shown in italics are those of people mentioned in letters but not the writers.

† *indicates the soldier died during the war.*

Frater, J., Lance-Corporal, 4th Battalion K.O.S.B. - p.55
Fleming, Jimmie - p.57
French, Sir John, Field Marshall i/c B.E.F. - p.27, p.28
Furness, J., Sergeant, 10th Battalion DL.I. † - p.32

Gittus, John, Bombardier, 1st Brigade R.F.A. (Ex Newcastle Fire Brigade) † - p.7
Gould, James, Private, 4th Battalion, Northumberland Fusiliers - p.32
Grey, Corporal, 5th Northumberland Fusiliers † - p.22

Hamilton, Sir Ian, General in command of the Mediterranean Expeditionary
    Force 1915 - p.50
Handyside, J. R., Bombardier, D Battery, 71st Brigade, R.F.A. † - p.49
Henderson, J., Private, 6th Battalion Manchester Regiment † - p.55

Iung, H. A., Second Lieutenant, Northumberland Fusiliers † - p.24

Johnson, John, Corporal, 4th Battalion Northumberland Fusiliers - p.70

Kelsey, Cis - p.17
Kitchener, Herbert, Field Marshall, Lord, Secretary of State for War - p.46

Macgregor, A. C., Private, Anson Battery, Royal Naval Division - p.50
Mattinson, Henry, Trooper, Northumberland Hussars - p.9, *p.9,* p.13
McLeod, George, Corporal, 7th Battalion Northumberland Fusiliers † - p.31
Michie, Henry, Trooper, Northumberland Hussars - p.9, *p.13*
Millerand, M., French Minister of War - p.46
Moor, D., Private 2nd Battalion Royal Inniskilling Fusiliers - p.40
Morgan, W., Private, D.L.I. † - p.49

Naisbet, Jack - p.57
Nash, Captain † - p.27

Pearce, I., Private. 5th Battalion D.L.I. - p.30, p.40
Peckard, Staff Sergeant, (Newcastle and Gateshead Gas Company) - p.67
Pratt, Thomas, Signaller, 5th Battalion, Northumberland Fusiliers - p.71
Proudfoot, John, Private, 2nd Battalion, K.O.S.B. - p.24

Quincey, A. E., Private, 2nd Battalion, D.L.I. - p.40

GLOSSARY

baby-killers:
nickname given to the German troops, based on accounts of atrocities they committed in Belgium in the early stages of the war. The nickname formed the basis of a famous British recruiting poster showing a German soldier bayoneting a baby.

bully or **bully beef**:
the name given to tins of corned beef. 'Bully' is supposedly the anglicisation of the French word 'bouilli' meaning 'boiled'.

gun-limber:
a horse drawn gun carriage.

heliograph:
a signalling system which uses a mirror to send morse code signals with flashes of sunlight.

Jack Johnson:
a nickname for a German shell which burst with black smoke. It was named after John Arthur Johnson, the first black American heavyweight boxing champion (1908-1915).

lyddite:
a form of high explosive, consisting of picric acid, used by the British in World War I.

sap; sappers:
sap comes from the French 'saper' to dig or trench, and in World War 1 usually refers to tunnels which the soldiers on both sides attempted to dig beneath enemy lines. Those who dug them were sappers, but more generally, since the mid nineteenth century, the term is used instead of 'private' for soldiers in the Royal Engineers.

Taube:
a monoplane originally used in Austria in 1910, and which by 1914 made up half the German air force. When the linen covered wings were painted with lacquer or dope, the plane became almost transparent and difficult to spot from the ground.

volplane:
a steep controlled dive or downward flight, generally without engine power.

whiz-bang:
a German shell fired from a high-velocity gun which gave soldiers no time to duck. It was named from its sound - the whizz of the shell coming through the air followed by the bang made by the gun which fired it.